W9-AGJ-746

Praise for *The Invisible*

The Invisible rings a bell for justice like the Salvation Army outside the shopping mall at Christmas. Arloa is persistent, and she is contagious. This book is brim full of good sermons, and Arloa's life is her best sermon. Here is a message that will ring hope in your ears whether you are in a small town in Iowa or the Southside of Chicago. Arloa's words are filled with the promise and the dare that we can all do something beautiful for God in response to the suffering of others. Arloa reminds us that when we ask God to do something about poverty, God is saying back to us, "I did do something. I made you."

—Shane Claiborne, author, activist, recovering sinner

Everything about the Arloa I have known for more than twenty years and now see in her book, *The Invisible*, breathes integrity. How could I not admire her rural-to-urban journey, her amazing resiliency over time, her capacity to live with chaos and ambiguities on every side? I was reminded on nearly every page that Arloa has been teachable—she can learn from nurturing little lambs on the farm to saving lives on city streets. Broken people on the journey have given her new lenses to see familiar Scriptures in new ways. Like the most famous urban ministry leader of my lifetime, Teresa of Calcutta, Arloa reminds me that God is using her in places and ways that totally transcend her race and gender. Not incidentally, she is also reminding me why Chicago is still the perfect lab and base for her teaching and writing. Idiosyncratic characters leap off the streets in her writing. Jesus has chosen to turn her pain and vulnerability into a power that transforms people and places.

—Ray Bakke, Chancellor, Bakke Graduate University

The Invisible makes God's people visible. I will never be the same after reading Arloa Sutter's words. She has forever changed my heart, redirected my passion, and moved me to action. Arloa is a brilliant champion of community, involvement, engagement, and truth! When it comes to transforming the face of poverty, her wisdom is essential to the conversation. Her life among the urban poor is a beautiful story of hope and reconciliation. From this place, she calls us to wrestle with the issues and be God's voice of change together.

—Rev. Tracey Bianchi, pastor for women at Christ Church of Oak Brook

Arloa is a passionate leader and advocate for the poor. Her life and work are an inspiration to me. *The Invisible* will inspire many to see and live out God's heart for "the least of these."

—Leroy Barber, President of Mission Year

If you want God to capture more of your heart, read this book. If you want God's presence to pour through your heart, read this book. If you want to join God where he is working, read this book. Arloa Sutter is a woman after God's own heart. From first-hand experience, I can tell you she is the real deal. She has faithfully communicated the heart of God for the poor for nearly twenty years, and the fruit produced can only be explained by acknowledging "God did it." This book wasn't written from an ivory tower, but from the hardened streets of Chicago. The stories that Arloa shares and the journey she describes are compelling. If you like true stories that inspire, read this book.

—Don Cousins, Bible teacher and author

The Invisible should be required reading for every person in America. Arloa Sutter has lived it—she knows the problems. Using God's words, she gives surprisingly simple answers to our recurring question about how to make a difference in the lives of people sorely in need of a blessing. You will never be able to look in the eyes of a homeless person again and ask yourself, *What will happen to me if I get involved?* Now it's, *What will happen to them if I don't?* Arloa reminds all Christians especially that (in the words of my friend and coauthor, Denver Moore), "We is all homeless . . . just a workin' our way home."

—Ron Hall, coauthor of *Same Kind of Different as Me*

I heartily recommend *The Invisible*. It is a vital resource for anyone looking to understand God's heart for the poor. One of the most encouraging trends I see today is the Christian church reawakening to God's timeless care and concern for the least and last among us. But an awakening without proper training can lead to tremendous frustration and pain for everyone involved. This book shows churches the way.

—Daniel Hill, senior pastor, River City Community Church

I've never met anyone quite like the author of this book, Arloa Sutter. Listen to her. She is a powerful force for the good—single-mindedly dedicated to improving the lives of the poor. The time I have spent with her has touched me deeply and changed the way I think about poverty and homelessness. If only there were more people like Arloa, the world would be a much better place.

—Steven Levitt, coauthor of *Freakonomics* and *Superfreakonomics*

The Invisible is a compelling personal journey from the Iowa countryside to the toughest streets of Chicago, leading Breakthrough (one of the most successful urban ministries of our times). It is Arloa Sutter's journey of faith into action—a journey enhanced along the way with true stories of people's transformation from poverty to meaningful life, from compassionate wealth at arm's length to meaningful and personal action. Arloa frankly tackles the questions we have about poverty, and with Scripture and gentle reason, she draws the reader through the journey into an active and full life. Read the book at your own risk . . . but risk that cannot lose, with faith that leads to life-changing action.

—Mary Nelson, president emeritus, Bethel New Life

The Invisible

The Invisible

What the Church Can Do to
Find and Serve the Least of These

Arloa Sutter

wesleyan
publishing
house

Indianapolis, Indiana

Copyright © 2010 by Arloa Sutter
Published by Wesleyan Publishing House
Indianapolis, Indiana 46250
Printed in the United States of America
ISBN: 978-0-89827-456-1

Library of Congress Cataloging-in-Publication Data

Sutter, Arloa.
  The invisible : finding and serving the least of these / Arloa Sutter.
    p. cm.
  Includes bibliographical references and index.
  ISBN 978-0-89827-456-1 (alk. paper)
  1. Church work with the poor. 2. Poverty--Religious aspects--Christianity. I. Title.
  BV639.P6.S87 2010
  259.086'942--dc22
                          2010015323

All Scripture quotations, unless otherwise indicated, are taken from the HOLY BIBLE, NEW INTERNATIONAL VERSION ®. NIV ®. Copyright 1973, 1978, 1984 by International Bible Society. Used by permission of Zondervan. All rights reserved.

Scripture quotations marked (KJV) are taken from THE HOLY BIBLE, KING JAMES VERSION.

Scripture quotations marked (TNIV) taken from the HOLY BIBLE, TODAY'S NEW INTERNATIONAL VERSION®. Copyright © 2001, 2005 by International Bible Society®. Used by permission of International Bible Society®. All rights reserved worldwide.

Scripture quotations marked (NKJV) are taken from the New King James Version. Copyright © 1982 by Thomas Nelson, Inc. Used by permission. All rights reserved.

Scripture quotations marked (NLT) are taken from the Holy Bible, New Living Translation, copyright 1996, 2004. Used by permission of Tyndale House Publishers, Inc., Wheaton, Illinois 60189. All rights reserved.

Scripture quotations marked (RSV) are taken from the Revised Standard Version of the Bible, copyright © 1946, 1952, and 1971 National Council of the Churches of Christ in the United States of America. Used by permission. All rights reserved.

Scripture quotations marked (MSG) are taken from *The Message*. Copyright © 1993, 1994, 1995, 1996, 2000, 2001, 2002. Used by permission of NavPress Publishing Group.

All rights reserved. No part of this publication may be reproduced, stored in a retrieval system, or transmitted in any form or by any means—electronic, mechanical, photocopy, recording or any other—except for brief quotations in printed reviews, without the prior written permission of the publisher.

For the past eighteen years, I have been privileged to walk alongside some of the most compassionate and resolute servants of Christ that I could ever hope to meet: the board, staff, and volunteers of Breakthrough Urban Ministries in Chicago, a ministry that has touched the lives of tens of thousands of Chicago's underprivileged, offering housing, food, shelter, education, health care, and counseling along with boatloads of personal love and affirmation. They have shown me the way of love and have been at the forefront of my personal transformation. This book is dedicated to them.

Contents

Acknowledgements

It seems like I have been writing this book all of my life, and in a sense, I have. Finally, the birthing process has come to an end and the baby is here. I have many people to thank.

My inner call to write took on urgency when Don Cousins led our Breakthrough board and leadership team in a strategic planning session in 2006. He looked me in the eyes and said, "You need to write a book." It sounded easy, and I assured the Breakthrough board that I would write it during my Christmas vacation that winter.

I asked my author friend Keri Wyatt Kent for help and began to flood her with stories. We stuck Post-it notes on the wall to try and organize them into a book, but they remained scrambled notes on paper. In desperation, I called Don Cousins and vented, "You said I should write a book, but I don't know what I'm supposed to write about."

His response set me on a course that brought structure out of my scrambled thoughts. He said, "We need a deeper theology about how to care for the poor. We all feel like we should do something. We want to care about the poor, but we don't know what to do. We know God loves the poor, and we should too, so, we organize a trip to Haiti or Mexico. We feel better for a while, but then we are left wondering if we really made a difference. We need to learn how to care for the poor, not out of guilt and obligation, but because God loves us and wants what's best for us."

That was it! I knew what I needed to do.

I spent some time away at Lonnie Bone's cabin in Ontario and at the Mianowanys' beach house in the Outer Banks of North Carolina and began to outline a structure that would address the dilemma Don had outlined. Another author friend, Dave Jackson, came alongside me to help me develop this final version of the book. I know now how much I needed Don, Keri, and Dave to set me on course and to encourage me to stay in the process. Thanks to Lonnie Bone and the Mianowanys for letting me write in such beautiful settings.

I also want to thank the board and staff of Breakthrough who continued to believe I could actually complete a book when I didn't get it done during my Christmas vacation in 2006. They have been patient, and it is their amazing work that keeps Breakthrough such a cutting-edge ministry that continues to generate inspiring stories of transformation. I love you all dearly.

Special thanks to the women of the Redbud Writers Guild. You are the kindest group of loving critics I have ever met. I am proud to be associated with you.

Carolyn, our long talks on the backpacking trails in Colorado have centered and inspired me. Thanks for giving me your "out of the box" perspectives. You help me keep it real.

Thanks to Ray Bakke, my longtime friend and mentor, who guided me in reflection and study in shantytowns and squatter villages in Manila, Hong Kong, China, and Ethiopia and created my doctorate of ministry program. Your commitment to bringing the whole gospel to the world has inspired me to open my heart to the poor across the world.

To Daniel Hill, my pastor at the River City Community Church, thanks for believing in me, for reading early manuscripts and assuring me it was worthwhile. I really appreciate your friendship and support.

Thanks to my agent, Sandra Bishop, and MacGregor Literary Agency, for believing this book had merit and taking on an aspiring author.

I am very pleased to be published with Wesleyan Publishing House. The Wesleyans have a long honorable history of advocating for the abolition of slavery and women's suffrage. Meeting the good folks at Wesleyan Publishing House and Dr. Jo Anne Lyon, General Superintendent of The Wesleyan Church, was like coming home for me.

My daughters, Teri and Monica, you know these stories are real. We lived them together. I'm so glad you are in my life. Thanks for letting me sit with my computer on my lap for countless hours. I'm proud of both of you, and, of course, Jayden and Naomi, my grandchildren, who teach me how to love and play as only children can.

Most of all, I want to thank the people whose stories I tell in this book: men and women who have made the courageous choice to step out of their chains of addiction, to embrace love after experiencing so much disappointment, and to go on day after day with scars of pain from abusive relationships and rejection. Thanks for teaching me so much about God's love. I am humbled to have known you and am inspired every day by your faith and courage. You have blessed me.

Foreword by Bob Lupton

There is a growing interest among people of faith to engage in service among the poor. It has become normative for churches, large and small, to schedule mission trips and service projects as part of their annual calendar of activities. Encounters with needy people have the potential to effect significant and lasting changes in the lives of those who volunteer to serve as well as those being served. Such changes, however, can be for better or for worse.

Those who sign up for mission trips or spend a night in a homeless shelter often return with glowing reports of how they have seen God at work in surprising ways in the lives of destitute people. They have seen faith where they expected to see despair, spiritual life where they assumed there would be only darkness. Their eyes have been opened to strange new manifestations of the kingdom. Just as often, however, others return confused. Troubling questions have arisen about the causes of poverty, about unhealthy dependency, and the ineffectiveness of charity. Too often such questions go unaddressed and negative stereotypes about the poor deepen.

Mission trips and service projects have become big business. More than two billion dollars was spent last year funding these ventures. At first appearance, this would seem to be an exciting new emphasis for the church—a renewed obedience to care for "the least of these" as our Lord instructed. However, to date, very little attention has been given to assessing the effectiveness of this service. Those on the receiving end tend to be less than candid for fear of losing the financial support churches bring. Seldom do volunteers hear that they have come across as patronizing, have caused more work than they have accomplished, or have fostered unhealthy dependency. Yet the church needs the candor and guidance of those on the receiving end if her service is to be ultimately redemptive.

There is another impediment to vital feedback from the recipient side. Frontline practitioners are so consumed with the day-to-day pressures of their calling that they seldom take time to write down their experiences. But over time, their daily lives become treasure troves of practical wisdom that is sorely needed by fresh troops coming to serve. Thus, the literature needed to guide the church into effective service among the poor is in short supply.

The Invisible has come off the press not a moment too soon. Arloa Sutter has chronicled two decades of her life among the homeless and destitute of inner-city Chicago. She has experienced devastating lows and exhilarating highs as she has faithfully followed her calling to live among broken people. Her insights are grounded in stark reality. Though her counsel is highly practical, she offers no simple remedies to the complexities of urban poverty.

What she does offer is unvarnished truth about service among the poor—what works and what hurts. Through powerful stories of her friends from the street, Arloa provides behind-the-scenes glimpses of a world seldom viewed by the achieving culture. What she learns from them—their survival struggles, their spiritual journeys, their perceptions of the world—she interprets for us. In so doing, she offers us highly valuable insights into how redemptive relationships can connect across the chasms of class and race.

I know something about the time, discipline, and emotional energy it requires to write a book such as this. I am so grateful to Arloa for carving out the many weekends and countless early-morning hours to produce a work of such great importance to the work of the kingdom in the city. Her contribution is enormous. I'm sure you will agree after you read it.

Foreword by Jo Anne Lyon

I met Arloa for the first time in something of a "meet and greet" context at the Christian Community Development Association annual convention. I immediately sensed her wisdom, passion, and leadership strengths. But it was through a longer conversation in my office some time later that I realized the depth of understanding and call Arloa was living out in the daily fabric of her life. She is about loving those who, in Jesus' words, are "the least of these." Listening to her made me hungry to learn and hear more.

The Invisible is doing just that for the church—making us hungry to know and do more for the least of these. Arloa connects with many of us evangelicals who rarely hear sermons that even mention God's heart for the poor. While we go on mission trips to the cities, or overseas, and make the poor the object of personal evangelism, we can be blind to any opportunity to have an ongoing relationship . . . to truly love them.

Arloa is transparent in her journey, both personally and professionally. Through a very difficult personal time when it seemed all stability in her life had been swept away, we witness her very vulnerable and human side. But finally, in a resolute moment, she writes in her journal, "I will not back down from my calling from God to minister in the city." You will be amazed to see what happens following her resolute "stake driven in the ground."

I greatly appreciate, too, the depth in which biblical theology is woven throughout the chapters in the book. This is not a "do-gooder" manual. This is soundly based on Scripture. In fact, the heart of the book could be used very effectively as a long-term study for various groups. I personally want to linger through this section to focus on what God is saying to the church and to me.

Arloa's courage and commitment are evident in her journey of several days as a homeless person. She gives us an opportunity to experience vicariously a bit of what it means to be homeless. Her experience adds new insight to the issues of powerlessness. Through such experiences, I believe we will be better able to understand the value of reciprocal relationships with the poor, which in turn become the foundation for building peace. In her words, "To do justice is to reweave the fabric of shalom, to go to those places where the fabric of society has unraveled and do what we can to repair it. We invest our time, energy, and money into society because it builds the shalom of God. The loss of neighborhood shalom eventually leads to crime, poverty, racial tension, and gang wars. This is not what God intended."

This is hard, tension-filled, never ending work. We sometimes hear the terms *compassion fatigue* or *compassion-burn-out*, and Arloa knows all about that. Her practice of not going it alone has been key to her journey. Her staff's mutual commitment and support is a model for many ministries. Indeed, they knew they were not able to go it alone either: They constantly stopped and listened to what God was saying. As one of them wrote on an easel pad once, "We must be led by the Spirit, rather than driven by need." This became the Word of the Lord to the staff. It takes discipline to live by this creed in such a need-based ministry. However, as I sat with Arloa in my office on that winter day, I realized the peace in her own soul, with which she reached out and touched me, was the outpouring of those words etched on that easel pad several years ago. She isn't going it alone—she does what she does with God and with his people.

I am asking you to read this book with a prayer that the Holy Spirit will speak to you with new insight and courage. I believe transformation of people and cities will take place through the people who read this book. I am eager to see the results.

Thank you, Arloa, for giving us this treasure from your life to be a mighty wave that keeps moving through the world, bringing God's justice, peace, and love.

Introduction

I am still haunted by the image: his gnarled face burned by the wind and sun; open sores festering on his cheeks; his sad sunken eyes imploring me at my car window. His dirt-crusted hand projected a McDonald's coffee cup under my nose while he balanced himself on one leg and a rag-wrapped crutch.

I'm not sure why it got to me this time, but something in me broke, and I began to weep. Instead of avoiding his eyes like I usually did, I gazed into them and seemed to soak his pain deep into my soul.

What if God had entrusted me with that body? What if I were forced to live day by day

> *The love of our neighbor is the only door out of the dungeon of self, where we mope and mow, striking sparks and rubbing phosphorescences out of the walls, and blowing our own breath in our own nostrils, instead of issuing to the fair sunlight of God, the sweet winds of the universe.*
>
> —George MacDonald

on the whims of charity, bills thrust at me so that I would go away to some burned-out basement or rat-riddled tunnel.

What difference would my little contribution make in this man's life? Did it really matter how I responded? Does anything I do really matter in the face of life-crippling poverty in our inner cities and in developing countries throughout the world?

The man at my car window forced me to face many perplexing issues that make me uncomfortable. I have struggled with my responsibility to men and women like him for years. It started shortly after I moved to the city and began to be confronted on a regular basis by panhandlers at the door of my local grocery store.

In a country dominated by affluence, where we have been assured in our Declaration of Independence that we are "endowed by [our] Creator with certain unalienable Rights, that among these are Life, Liberty and the pursuit of Happiness," why are there thousands of people who are in obvious distress forced to stand on street corners, begging for their very existence?

What is broken in our system of justice that would force a coterie of broken-down, worn-out, and wounded people to suffer at the side of the road, unable to find sustainable income to survive without reaching out for charity from detached, dispassionate passersby? What, if anything, can I do that will make a difference?

Since this man had somehow touched a well of compassion deep within me, I reached in my wallet and pulled out the only bill I found there, a twenty. The man's eyes lit up when he saw the bill, but I was still troubled. Twenty dollars was nothing in the face of this man's need. Where was his family? What was his story? Was anyone willing to walk alongside this man to make sure he had proper care? Was anyone available to him to listen to his story and to show him the love of God?

Many of us struggle with our responsibility to the poor. Is it okay for me to have what I have and live where I live? Is giving money an appropriate response, and if so, how much and to whom? Must I, like the rich young ruler of Scripture, give all I own to the poor in order to follow Jesus? Should I be selling everything and moving into an inner-city ghetto or to India or Africa? Is God pleased with how I am living? What, if anything, that I do will make a difference?

This book is an attempt to grapple with those questions. It is a journey into the pain of the man at my car window. It is my attempt to add to the discussion that is rising in the church about the suffering of the three billion people in the world living in abject poverty and how their struggles shape the way we live.

I want you to know from the outset that I am writing this book with my hand over my mouth. What do I mean by that?

There is an unnerving story in the Old Testament about a man named Job who faced an onslaught of trouble. His friends tried to grapple with his suffering, but when they opened their mouths, they revealed their ignorance. Job tried in vain to reply to their insults until finally God intervened and let out a two-chapter rant.

"Where were you when I laid the earth's foundation?" God questioned. "Tell me if you understand. . . . Have you ever given orders to the morning, or shown the dawn its place? . . . Do you know when the mountain goats give birth? . . . Do you give the horse his strength?" (Job 38:4, 12; 39:1, 19).

Finally, Job said, "I am unworthy—how can I reply to you? I put my hand over my mouth" (Job 40:4). He relented. Whereupon God went on with the rant for two more chapters.

So, I, too, put my hand over my mouth and venture to write about a subject that is complicated, uncomfortable, perplexing, and perhaps even threatening. I pray that, at the least, it will generate conversations that will move you toward compassion and justice for the poor and a deeper understanding of God's love for all people and for you.

With my hand over my mouth, I write this book to pour my stories into the ever-widening stream of consciousness about God's transforming, redemptive love and hope for the world. I also want to implore my brothers and sisters in Christ to take a fresh look at our individual and corporate responses to the cry of the poor among us.

As I have walked for the past eighteen years alongside thousands of men and women who have become homeless in the city of Chicago, and as I have visited impoverished communities throughout the world, I have discovered good news. We actually can, in very practical ways, find sustainable, manageable ways to make a difference in the lives of the poor.

I have also discovered a hidden mystery: When we engage in the lives of the poor, our lives are changed as well. We are transformed in ways we never would have dreamed possible. Indeed, through my eighteen-year ministry with Breakthrough Urban Ministries in Chicago, I have experienced radical personal transformation. This book is about that journey.

I am writing from a deep-seated passion for the Christian church. A growing group of Christians are awakening toward the values of justice, compassion, reconciliation, and community renewal. Some of these awakenings have been spiritual in nature, as people have come to recognize God's heart throughout Scripture for the centrality of these values. Some of these awakenings have been social in nature, inspired and provoked by the significant changes in society, including globalization and the election of an African-American president who cut his teeth as a community organizer in inner-city Chicago.

This book will build on the awakening that is happening in circles around our country. Through stories, real-life examples, theological and philosophical models, and practical instruction, my prayer is that you will experience breakthroughs that will move you along a continuum toward a lifestyle characterized by compassion and justice for the poor. My desire is that we will join together to make life-transforming decisions that will change the world and bring us closer to the heart of God for the poor and that we will know what it means to be moved by the love of Christ in relationship to them.

By picking up this book, you are making the brave choice to move forward in a journey toward engaging more meaningfully with the poor. This book will serve as a tool that will spur you on in your journey toward making more choices that will touch your heart with the compassion of Christ.

Perhaps you are well on your way toward understanding what it means to follow Jesus to the poor. It is my prayer that this book will open the door of your thinking to new perspectives that will cauterize your resolve and reaffirm your commitment to the poor.

We are not in this journey alone. We join a great throng of heroes who can show us the way. From the prophets of the Old Testament of Scripture, to St. Francis of Assisi, William Wilberforce, John Wesley, Dorothy Day, Mother Teresa, and modern-day practitioners and prophets such as John Perkins, Shane Claiborne, Wayne Gordon, and Bob Lupton, we have guides who can help us in our journey to the poor.

I have also had the privilege to walk alongside some of the most compassionate and resolute servants of Christ that I could ever hope to meet: the board, staff, and volunteers of Breakthrough Urban Ministries in Chicago, a ministry that has touched the lives of tens of thousands of Chicago's underprivileged, offering housing, food, shelter, education, health care, and counseling along with boatloads of personal love and affirmation. They have shown me the way of love and have been at the forefront of my personal transformation.

The Christian church is the largest grassroots movement on earth. How we respond to people like the man at my car window is central to the life and teachings of Jesus and what it means for us to follow Christ. Together we can make a profound impact on poverty. Indeed, I believe we are called by God to do so.

My Journey to the City

Sitting in my family's '67 Rambler on a clear, star-filled night in George, Iowa, I turned the dial of the car radio until I found WLS, a music station from Chicago. My spirit was mesmerized by the pounding energy of the city. Something inside drew me irresistibly to merge myself with the ongoing struggle for the soul of the city. I knew someday I would be there.

There was a rhythmic simplicity to my life on the farm. I created a little rhyme that I sang as I milked the family cow each morning and evening. "Here flows the milk. Swish. There flows the milk. Swish . . ." I sang it over and over to the rhythm of my right and left squeeze until the milk pail filled with the frothy gift of life from Bessy, who, apart from an occasional kick

> *Some people want to live within the sounds of chapel bells. I want to run a mission a yard from the gates of hell.*
>
> —C. T. Studd

and whip of the tail to detach pesky flies from her hide, stood in compliant cooperation.

Bessy released her gift, first to her calf, who had subsequently grown apart from her, and now to our family. We would skim off the cream and whip it with sugar to top homemade pies. We would churn it into butter and crank it into rich ice cream. We would pour it over blueberries and stir it with chocolate until our hips bulged and our livers smiled. I knew inherently that the Almighty, the creator and sustainer of the universe, meant for there to be a nourishing flow of milk and honey, a delightful balance of sweetness and energy, to carry us through life until we died with smiles on our faces, received into glory with a benevolent pat on the back for a life well lived.

Yet there was a disquieting rumble pecking insistently at my worldview. Like a disturbing rash, I couldn't stop its itching. It emerged from *Life* magazine in the battered face of Emmit Till, a boy whose brutal murder gave a strong impetus to the American civil rights movement. With Emmit's broken body lying grotesquely in a coffin, thousands paraded by him in heart-wrenching protest for the thousands of others who had been snatched violently away without the notice of the world. The silent parade screamed all the way to my quiet world in rural Iowa that the black population had had enough of the deadly consequences of fear and prejudice. Something was terribly wrong with the world.

It leapt out at me from the little black and white TV my parents finally allowed. I saw neighborhoods burn while police and firemen stood by in fear, and as rage and despair swept through the African-American community after the death of Dr. Martin Luther King, Jr. Though I was miles away geographically and experientially, I began to identify with the pain in the faces of people I saw on the screen. The injustice was obvious to me, and I couldn't imagine why a group of human beings could face such inhumane treatment.

It lured me through the desperate pleas of Thomas Dorsey as I learned to haltingly play on the piano the somber chords of "Precious Lord, take my hand, lead me on, help me stand—I am tired, I am weak, I am worn." Somehow, I knew the Lord was going to respond to the pleas of those who sang that song from the depths of their being, and I wanted to join them in their lament and experience deliverance alongside them.

The painful, throbbing cry of the poor in the city was far away and foreign to me, yet I couldn't shake its call. The contrast of the cry of the urban poor with the comfortable life I saw around me in my small-town farming community produced in me, in the words of Bill Hybels, "a holy discontent."[1] It just didn't make sense for there to be such disparities.

If Jesus wanted to redeem the world, wouldn't he care most deeply about those places where his dear ones wept over the premature deaths of their children, where they struggled for food, clothing, and shelter? Wouldn't he want to be there with them when they felt hopeless and discouraged? Wouldn't God want to reach out to encourage and support them? If God was truly a God of love—if, in fact, God was love itself—wouldn't the Almighty want to bring the river of abundant life to dry parched places?

I believed that the light of Christ should be taken to the darkest places on the planet and the city seemed to be such a place, a place where many lived in great need. I felt the tug of God on my heart that moved me away from the secure nest of my life on the farm to venture into the unknown, the big city, where my life would never be the same.

The quote mentioned earlier said, "Some people want to live within the sounds of chapel bells. I want to run a mission a yard from the gates of hell." These words capture the call of God for us to move out of our isolated cocoons and to go to the difficult places of the world where we find God most powerfully at work.

My experience in the city has not been that of being "a yard from the gates of hell" (well, maybe sometimes). For the most part, I have found God profoundly at work in the city, restoring it to wholeness through mothers who have been praying for years for their sons and grandsons; through tenacious school teachers who continue to believe in their students despite multiple failures, disappointments, and inadequate resources to help them; and through the homeless man who shares his last cigarette with a fellow stranger.

From an Iowa Farm to Inner-City Chicago

My great-grandparents came to America from Germany. They were stoic, hardworking Lutherans and Presbyterians who journeyed in the late 1800s by horse and buggy from Chicago to Freeport, Illinois, and then on to northwest Iowa. There they managed to purchase a quarter section, one hundred sixty acres of farmland. My father subsequently bought the land from his only brother, and for more than a hundred years, the Monkemeier family made a modest but adequate living growing corn, soybeans, and alfalfa; raising chickens, pigs, and cattle for market; milking cows; and shearing sheep. We were not wealthy, but we were landowners, and we always had plenty of fresh meat and garden vegetables to eat.

Our family epitomized the Protestant work ethic. Everyone in our family was expected to work hard, to make the most of what we had, and to live simply. We all had daily chores and were taught to do our part of the farm work as soon as we could walk.

While I was just a young child, my father grew more and more disabled with arthritis. By the time he was thirty, he had to give up his cow-milking enterprise. While his peers were busy buying more farmland and expensive tractors worth more than their houses, my father was selling equipment to get medical treatments. He loved farming and didn't want to give it up, so he welded iron steps up to his John Deere tractor seat. Every morning during the planting and harvest seasons, I would help by pushing him up the steps to the seat where he would sit all day until after sunset when I would help him back down. He kept farming for nearly twenty years despite his disability and then began to receive Social Security disability checks.

Despite our ultimate reliance on Social Security, I learned very early in life about the value of hard work and responsibility. I also saw the power of community as the neighboring farmers would join to help one another during hay-baling season. One fall when my father was bedridden because of his illness, the neighbors put together a row of ten combine harvesters and brought in his crop in one day.

Nearly everyone in my little hometown of George, Iowa, was of German descent. I didn't meet a person of color until a missionary brought a native-born African to our little church when I was ten. This experience fostered the notion that people who didn't look or act like me were certainly lost and in need of salvation. They were the objects of our missionary work. When I went to live and minister in an impoverished community in the city of Chicago, I was surprised to learn that God was already at work there.

The many missionaries who passed through often stayed in our home. They gave me a deep appreciation for sharing the gospel cross-culturally. I was inspired by their stories of courage and improvisation. I remember hearing about Frank Drown, a missionary who used nearly every piece of a fallen airplane in the jungle of Bolivia to better the lives of the villagers. He used the metal from the plane to build a water tower that provided running water for the village. I was impressed by his passion to not only share the good news of eternal salvation but to raise the quality of their day-to-day lives.

The Bible church our family attended fostered in me a love for Scripture and a deep familiarity with it. I learned, however, a focus on selected verses of the Bible. While I knew the Bible well as a child, I somehow missed the many passages of Scripture that speak about the poor and our responsibility toward them. I don't remember one sermon that mentioned God's heart for the poor.

Once or twice a year, volunteers from our church led a service at a gospel mission in a city in nearby South Dakota. The skid-row neighborhood of the city was very different from what I was accustomed to in my farming community. We brought our church's latest special music, duets, and trios. Occasionally I even played my flute. Our pastor would preach a message about personal salvation. There was always an alter call with "Just As I Am" playing in the background.

The men looked very bored by our little program. Most sat as far in the back of the auditorium as they could, and many smelled of alcohol. We never actually spoke with any of them. They would sit through the service in order to eat the soup and bread that followed and get a night inside from the wintry South Dakota cold. Even then I wondered if what we were doing really made a difference in their lives. There had to be a better way.

During the summers of my last two years of high school, I joined a group of students from Canada to help one of our church's missionaries in the inner city of St. Louis. We stayed with the missionary in a nice suburban home. Every weekday morning, we would pile into his Lincoln Continental and drive into the city to teach vacation Bible school in black churches to the kids. Then we would drive back out to the suburbs and relax. I remember the contrasts: the smells of the kids in the sweltering St. Louis summer heat, the barrenness of the neighborhoods, and the curiosity of those who loved to touch my hair.

After high school, I eagerly enrolled at Moody Bible Institute in Chicago. I brought a bike and spent many hours riding through the various ethnic neighborhoods, amazed by the richness of the cultural contrasts. In my first year at Moody, one of my assignments was to teach Sunday school in the Dearborn Homes, a Chicago Housing Authority project on the Near South Side, near 30th and State streets. I taught on Sunday mornings with Bertha Harris, an elderly resident of the projects who built relationships with the children in the community by selling candy and inviting them to Sunday school in the building's community room.

I was stunned to experience the bleak living conditions in the projects: elevators that smelled of urine, graffiti on the walls, bars and chains on the doors, and burned-out garbage chutes. As I traveled by subway and then the elevated CTA (Chicago Transit Authority) train, I would watch as the white people from the north side of Chicago exited the train at the downtown exits, and the black people got on. By the time I made it to my stop at 31st Street, I would be the only white person on the train. It was frightening to exit the train and walk into the neighborhood of the infamous Robert Taylor Homes. Ms. Harris would wait for me at the stop and drive me the few blocks north to the Dearborn Homes so I wouldn't have to walk through the projects to get there.

Another one of my Moody assignments was a semester of nursing home visitation. I was sent to a bleak Medicare home where all of the residents were very poor. Rather than moving from room to room, I latched on to Emma, a tiny, elderly, African-American woman in a wheelchair. I visited her every week for the entire semester, reading to her from the Bible and praying with her. One of her legs had been amputated, and one of her eyeballs was missing from its socket. She was totally blind. She didn't speak to me much, but her only eye would drip tears when I came, and she would clutch my hand as I read to her and prayed. Emma asked me to read Psalm 23 over and over.

On the very last day of my assignment, I went to Emma's room as usual and was confused not to see her sitting at her door in her wheelchair. Her bed was neatly made. As I stood there bewildered, a nurse asked me if I was Arloa. "Yes," I replied, "I'm looking for Emma."

"Honey, she died yesterday," the nurse told me sympathetically. "Here, she wanted you to have this. It was all she had." The nurse handed me a little purse with a picture inside of Emma as a young girl with her brother.

I had no idea that I was Emma's only friend, the only one who spoke with her, prayed for her, and touched her. I wondered how many more Emmas there were at that home and at the many other homes across the city. My heart was stirred by the plight of those who had been deserted and forgotten.

Mother Teresa said, "The biggest disease today is not leprosy or tuberculosis, but rather the feeling of being unwanted, uncared for, and deserted by everybody. We can cure physical diseases with medicine, but the only cure for loneliness, despair, and hopelessness is love."[2] Knowing that I was Emma's only earthly friend affected me deeply.

One summer, between semesters at Moody, I stayed in the city to work at the Garrett Popcorn Shop in the Loop. I would often work until closing at midnight and then walk a mile home to the apartment I shared with some friends. One night, I went into a doughnut shop after work and noticed an elderly woman sitting there with several shopping bags and a pile of newspapers. She wore layers of dresses and a pair of tattered pantyhose. I approached her and asked her what she was doing. She was working crossword puzzles.

She told me her name was Beatrice and that she would hang out at the doughnut shop until early morning when she would catch the Clark 22 bus to travel to a house in Andersonville, a neighborhood north of downtown. A man there would let her in and exchanged her cleaning services for the opportunity to sleep on a sofa for a few hours. When he returned from work, Beatrice would get back on the bus and return to the doughnut shop for another night.

As I listened to this woman's story, it occurred to me that the homeless were real people. She had a name and a life, and a routine. Her life was very different from mine, and yet, our paths had crossed that late night, and talking with her for several hours opened me up to a whole other world that intrigued and beckoned me to understand it.

The Early Years of Ministry

Upon my graduation from Moody, I took a position with Youth for Christ and their Juvenile Justice ministry. For four years, I met with groups of young girls who were in crisis. I loved taking them hiking, cross-country skiing, spelunking, and leading them to faith in Christ. I was unaware at the time of my own codependent tendencies. It felt good to be needed, and I found myself pulled into the drama of their lives. I would get calls in the middle of the night to pick up one of the girls who had passed out drunk in an alley or to negotiate a family dispute. I called 911 in desperation as a young woman overdosed on my living room floor. By the end of four years, I was exhausted. I cringed every time the phone rang for fear of hearing about another suicide attempt.

I know now that much of my early energetic zeal was rooted in my own pride and need. I had entered ministry recognizing my need for a Savior, but then attempted to rescue and save others in my own strength on behalf of the Savior. My work was compelling: girls in need, in pain, and in trouble, looking for me to rescue them. Eventually I worked myself to exhaustion. This experience of burnout would forever change my approach to ministry as I learned the importance of waiting on God in contemplation before rushing in with my own agenda, to be led by the Spirit instead of driven by need. I will discuss this in more detail in chapter 8.

While working with Youth For Christ (YFC), I met my soon-to-be husband who was attending Trinity Seminary to prepare for the pastorate. Since the churches I had been attending did not affirm women in ministry, the notion of serving the Lord as a pastor's wife suited me well. Sensing a call to urban ministry, after our marriage, we decided to move into the city of Chicago. I left my post at YFC and began hanging wallpaper and driving an ambulance in Chicago to help support the family while he finished his master's of divinity degree. We found a church home at the First Evangelical Free Church on the north side of Chicago.

Shortly after my first daughter was born in 1981, my husband took a pastorate position in Keokuk, Iowa, a small industrial town on the Mississippi River. I loved working in the church. I started a thriving children's program, and the church attendance steadily grew until we were able to buy land to build a new facility on the edge of town. I had another daughter, continued to hang wallpaper on the side, and finished my undergraduate degree in sociology at Western Illinois University in Macomb, Illinois.

The Call to the City

After nearly five years in the ministry in Keokuk, I asked my husband where he saw himself in the future. He remarked that he still longed to be in a thriving church in the city. I asked him what kind of neighborhood he imagined, and he said a neighborhood similar to that of First Free, where we had attended when we lived in Chicago. To our surprise, within a few months of that discussion we got a call from the search committee at First Free. We were unaware that they were in a search process for a new pastor.

Although we were happy in our comfortable church in Iowa, the phone call was clearly beyond coincidence. We moved forward with their invitations and soon accepted the call to pastor the First Evangelical Free Church in Chicago. With our two daughters, ages six and three, we moved back to Chicago. It was the fulfillment of a dream for me. I was finally involved with ministry in the city, in a church that was recommitting itself to its community.

I continued my work with children and organized a club for kids in the community. I began teaching a weekly women's Bible study and organized a moms' prayer group. I enjoyed my volunteer work with the church and managed to complete a master's degree in urban mission through an urban extension program of Lincoln Christian University.

After three years of ministry at First Free, my husband began telling me about an issue the church was facing. The church staff didn't know what to do about the many people who were coming to the church office throughout the week asking for assistance. Our church administrator had a big heart and was spending inordinate amounts of time listening to their stories and trying to decide how to help them. He always had a pot of coffee in the church office, and people from the street would often come and hang out with him there.

One day, I was in the office when Michael came in and asked for money for a security deposit on an apartment. His clothes were dirty, and he smelled of alcohol and urine. His afro was long overdue for a trim. I knew he was not likely to get housing looking like he did. He was happy to accept my suggestion for a shower in the bathroom in my husband's office. I found a set of fresh clothing for him from a bag of donations someone had dropped off, and I trimmed his hair in the church office kitchen. His shower, haircut, and clean clothing helped him look much more presentable, but his drinking problem would still keep him from getting what he needed. I recognized that his issues were much deeper than just getting cleaned up on the surface. What could we do for him that would really make a difference?

On another occasion, an elderly man rang the doorbell of the church office and made his way slowly up the long flight of stairs. He seemed a bit disoriented. "Could someone from the church help me move?" The man we later came to know as Robert implored, "I don't have enough money to hire movers. I live just half a block away."

I called Jim, a seminary intern, for help, and that afternoon we hauled all of Robert's belongings from his studio apartment down three flights of stairs and loaded them into the church van. Jim took the driver's seat as the three of us got into the van. "Okay, where to?" he asked.

Robert looked at him in desperation. "I don't know," he said. Robert, in his confusion, had not paid his rent for several months. When he got his eviction notice, he came to the church for help to move, but he had nowhere to go. Before our very eyes, Robert had become homeless.

And there was Brandy, a fourteen-year-old girl, brought in by a member of the church who had found her crying on a street corner near the church building. Brandy's mother decided she needed a break, so she gave Brandy bus fare and told her to go stay with her aunt for a couple of weeks. At the end of the visit, Brandy's aunt gave her bus fare and told her it was time for her to go back home. Brandy took the bus back to our neighborhood and went to the door of her home to find that her mother had moved and hadn't bothered to tell her where she had gone. Brandy was abandoned and alone in the city and terribly frightened. After we calmed Brandy down, she was able to tell us which school she had attended. A teacher helped us track down Brandy's mother so we could reunite them.

The Ministry of Breakthrough Is Birthed

When my two daughters were in school all day and I had some time to offer, I asked the church for permission to open a little storefront room that was being used as the church library. With the assistance of one of the recovering alcoholics who had been hanging out in the church office, I put on a pot of coffee and asked people from the church to provide soup, sandwiches, or spaghetti at noon, so I could welcome these wanderers in from the cold and take the time to get to know them. It wasn't long before word got out and the little room began to fill with men and women in search of safety and meaningful relationships.

I gathered a group of caring men and women from the church to form a board of directors, and in 1992, we incorporated Breakthrough Urban Ministries. After I sent letters to my Christmas card mailing list telling stories of the people I met, donations began coming in for the ministry.

I didn't know anything about forming an organization or about the established world of "homeless services," but the call I felt in rural Iowa gave birth to a ministry whose staff would walk alongside tens of thousands of homeless men and women, providing food, shelter and housing, and life-transforming relationships for people from very diverse backgrounds.

Six months after we opened our doors, I was joined by Judy Cuchetto. Judy had studied addictions counseling and taught me much about the practice of tough love for our guests. She helped to create a warm and inviting center and convinced her husband and son to come in on a Saturday to install a washer and dryer and shower in the back room of our little storefront. The board decided to start paying Judy and me a small salary from the donations we were receiving.

We always felt it was more dignifying to pay our guests for work they did rather than to simply provide handouts. When people would ask me for cash assistance to get a state ID or to rent a room, I would ask them to pick up trash along the Clark Street business district behind our church. Most were happy to have work and get paid. One day, the president of the local Chamber of Commerce noticed people picking up trash and asked questions that led her to come to me. She asked if the chamber could pay us to hire homeless men and women to clean the streets on a regular basis. I thought about it for a couple of seconds, and we wrote up a quick contract. Soon we were able to negotiate similar contracts in other neighborhoods, and Breakthrough was able to provide actual jobs and employment services for our guests.

A representative from the city heard about what we were doing and dropped in for a visit. As I gave her a tour of the facilities, she mentioned that the city would provide mats and pay us a per diem rate if we would open up our church gymnasium as a shelter for men. In 1994, we contracted with the city and began sheltering thirty men per night on the church gymnasium floor.

During a strategic planning session in 1998, we decided that we were being led to expand our services to accommodate homeless women. Since we were sheltering men, our services at First Free had become dominated by men. Women felt uncomfortable coming to our day center. I sent out a letter to our donors asking for prayer in our search for a building to serve women.

A few days later, I got a call from a policeman friend who said, "I've found your building." Through his police work on the west side of

Chicago, he had met a pastor who was operating a shelter out of a dilapidated factory building in the East Garfield Park neighborhood on Chicago's west side. The pastor was recovering from heart surgery and had decided he needed to give up his shelter work. He had posted a for sale sign on the building.

I met with the pastor and he agreed to lease the building to us at a nominal rate if we would renovate it and use it for ministry. A church in the suburbs decided to help fund the renovations, and in 2000, we opened a shelter for women in the building we now call the Breakthrough Joshua Center for Women.

When I went door to door in the community to win the support of the neighbors for our shelter for women, it became clear to me that the most pressing concern the community felt was for their children. Gangs and drug dealers ruled the streets, and the children had no safe place to go to after school. When a young couple, Bill and Marcie Curry, came to me with an idea to start a youth program, I enlisted them to join the Breakthrough staff, and we began working with children and their families in East Garfield Park.

As I listened to the stories of the men, women, and children who arrived at the doors of our shelters, I began to grow in my understanding of the devastating effects of the systemic issues of racism, poverty, and social injustice. My heart was broken by the stories of neglect and abuse many of them had experienced, and I became increasingly committed to the call of God on my life to organize a group of people who would look out for them and work for understanding and justice on their behalf.

My World Falls Apart

As the ministry of Breakthrough was flourishing, I was devastated to learn that my husband of nearly twenty years had decided to leave me and our family. Since my foremost identity and life work was wrapped up in being a pastor's wife, I was sure my ministry had come to an end. I contemplated resigning from my post at Breakthrough. What would I do? Where would I go? How would I support myself and my two children? Should I get out my wallpapering equipment again, return to driving an ambulance, go live with my mother? I was lost and confused.

I sought counseling and poured out my aching heart to my therapist and close friends. I built a little altar in my bedroom with candles and oil and cried before the Lord day after day. I read the classic daily devotional *My Utmost for His Highest*, hanging on every word from Oswald Chambers about God's love for me. Somehow, in the midst of the pain, I heard God say to me lovingly, "This, too, is for you." It seemed ludicrous to me! How could God use this devastating experience? I was broken and had no idea how to put the pieces of my life back together.

I wrote in my journal, "God is teaching me to sit in the pain; to sit under the heavy hand of God and let the pain do its work in me. I am having good talks with friends and good walks along the lake. The Lord has been very direct and tender with me. I am learning to 'let go and let God.' I strive to place my family in God's hands when I feel angry, anxious, or vengeful.

"I am also learning to be tenacious for truth. I have been duped, naïve. I have not been realistic about my own capacity for evil and that of others. I will be honest and expect honesty." At the advice of my counselors, I decided to stay the course and make life as stable as I could for my girls who, by then, were teenagers.

I struggled to understand how this could be part of God's plan for my life. The only way to get through the pain was to take one day at a time. For months, I could barely get out of bed, let alone lead a growing ministry in the city. While the Breakthrough board affirmed my continued leadership, I delegated much of the work I had been doing to others and focused on holding my family together. I wrote, "I will continue my involvement with Breakthrough as long as God allows. I will not back down from my calling from God to minister in the city."

I read a book by Gerald May titled *The Awakened Heart*. He suggested having a heart prayer, a word, phrase, or mental image that can bring us to the place of intimacy with Jesus in an instant. I knew immediately that my heart prayer image was the picture of Jesus, with nail scars in his hands, holding a little lamb to his breast.

The picture was vivid in my memory from an experience I had as a child when I stumbled over the frozen body of a lamb. Our buck had gotten out of his pen at the wrong time of the year, and in the middle of the winter, our sheep were giving birth to baby lambs and leaving them to die in the harsh winter cold. It was early in the morning, cold and dark, when I picked up the body of the dead lamb to place him on the growing pile of lambs for the rendering truck to pick up.

To my amazement, as I held the frozen lamb in my arms, I felt something I didn't expect. It was a warm breath from the lamb's nostrils! He was alive! I rushed him into the house, placed him in a box on a heat register, and began to rub him with warm towels. He remained stiff and cold.

I finally went into the kitchen to get a drink of water and I heard his strong, "Bah!" I rushed back to the heat register to find him standing up in his box, very much alive! I fed him with a nipple on a pop bottle and he followed me around like I was his mother.

Encouraged by the new life of that little lamb, I took on a crusade to save the lambs. I decided it was my job to rescue the other lambs that were being born in the frigid temperatures. Determined not to let another lamb die, I sat out in the barn at night and waited for the next mother to give birth to her baby. A pregnant ewe stomped her feet at me in pain and anger. I watched as she laid on her side moaning in childbirth and laboriously pushed out a new lamb. After the birth, she sniffed at her baby still kicking in his sack, and as if she knew the lamb would succumb to the cold temperatures, she walked away, abandoning him to the cold.

The mother stomped at me as I went over and picked up the wet little lamb. I brought him to my straw bed. I brushed off the mucous sack with my gloved hand, wiped his wool to a fluff with rags, and held him in my arms.

That image became my heart prayer. I prayed it often when I was fearful or doubtful, and God comforted me. In my imagination, I knew I was that little lamb. I needed to be rescued. I could not pull myself out of my suffocating sack of depression and despair. I needed the Savior, the Shepherd with nail scars in his hands, to bring me to a place of love and security, to hold me lovingly in his arms and restore me to life.

In my brokenness, I realized I am no different than the men and women who were coming to Breakthrough. I, too, am a single mother, struggling to survive and to find my way. I needed to be rescued by God and God's people. I needed (and still need) the community of faith for support. I would never be the same self-assured know-it-all.

I can relate to Naomi, a woman who never expected to be homeless. She held down two jobs and was paying her rent faithfully even after her husband died. When her landlord told her he was selling her building, and she would have to move out because the new owner wanted to turn the building into condos, Naomi thought she would just be able to rent another apartment.

She was surprised to learn that every landlord she approached turned down her requests for a lease, because she had never established credit. Not wanting to be a burden, she started living in her car. For over a year, she lived in her car without telling her grown children because she was embarrassed. When they called her on her cell phone, they had no idea she was sleeping in her car.

Naomi finally found her way to Breakthrough. One night she got up at 1:00 a.m. so she could be alone in the shower. She told me that as she stood in the shower, she began to weep and couldn't stop. She wept first of all in gratitude that she was able to take a shower, but more importantly because she recognized God had to put her in a homeless shelter for her not to look down on homeless people, for her not to think they were just lazy and didn't want to work. God put her there so she could experience his love.

Without the loving support of people in my life, I, too, could have been homeless. I learned to appreciate the family of God and their love for me, and would never again look at people in difficult circumstances from a condescending point of view. God allowed me to experience my own brokenness so I could experience God's love more profoundly. The Breakthrough family continued to love and support me and kept me sane. I thank God every day that somehow, through many tough challenges, God has kept me in ministry and given me the opportunity to continue my life work with Breakthrough.

Amazingly, it was during those years that Breakthrough grew much stronger and became even more fruitful. I learned the value of delegation and team building the hard way. The ministry became much more effective when I got out of the way and began to recruit strong leaders to take increasing responsibility.

The Move to East Garfield Park

In 2008, Breakthrough completed renovating another building near our Joshua Center for Women and moved our men's services and administrative offices into the East Garfield Park neighborhood on Chicago's west side.

The neighborhood of East Garfield Park was abandoned by white people in the fifties and sixties. Today, 97 percent of the residents are African-Americans. After the assassination of Rev. Martin Luther King, Jr., in 1968, many of the businesses and residences burned as casualties of the rage of community residents against "the man," the wealthy slum landlords who had let the buildings deteriorate. One out of every three lots in the neighborhood is vacant, a stark reminder of the lack of resources.

A full 38 percent of the residents of East Garfield Park live in poverty.[3] The unemployment rate in the community is 23 percent, nearly triple the city's average.[4] These conditions breed violence as many residents resort to illegal activities such as prostitution, gangs, and drug trafficking to survive. East Garfield Park has one of the highest homicide rates in the city of Chicago. It is one of three Chicago neighborhoods that receive 34 percent of Illinois' residents released from prison, nearly a thousand every year. Only 0.1 percent of those released from prison to the community are able to show the parole board or other authority a home or a plan for employment after their release. Employment opportunities are limited for those with a criminal record and an inadequate education.

Children and young people in the community have very few safe places to go. In the 2008–2009 school year, thirty-six Chicago Public School children were killed on the streets, most of them by gunfire. Chicago Public School children also have very limited opportunities for academic success. Only 37 percent of African-American boys in Chicago graduate from high school. Fewer than 5 percent attend college. Of those who drop out of high school, 68 percent are incarcerated by age twenty. The spiral of poverty is devastating for individuals, families, and the community of East Garfield Park.

After both of my daughters were grown, I moved into a little apartment in East Garfield Park. A month after I moved in, I was initiated into the neighborhood when a bullet went through my living room window and lodged in my dining room wall. I have never felt in danger personally in the neighborhood, but I recognize the convoluted challenges my neighbors experience daily, and my heart is continuing to soften as I grow more in touch with their struggles.

When you live in a neighborhood like mine, something happens. You begin to care about the broken school systems and the lack of employment opportunities for the people. You begin to identify with the people who are now your neighbors. Their concerns become your concerns.

As I entered my neighborhood Walgreens drugstore recently, I was asked for money three times from people who were struggling economically. As I arrived at the checkout counter, I waited while an inebriated man tried to pay with a personal check. He had to write it several times, first because he thought he was at Osco instead of Walgreens and then because he couldn't spell the name of the store.

I thought about how frustrated I would have been just a few years ago, disgusted with the desperation around me and the ignorance and folly of the uneducated, drunken man who was holding up the line. Instead, I find myself grieving and growing in compassion. My involvement with our homeless guests at Breakthrough has changed me. I still get tired and impatient, but learning the stories behind the struggles is softening my heart. I know that Jesus is growing me as I learn to love people and to suffer with them instead of judging them.

God has called me to live and work in an impoverished community in the city of Chicago. It is not a burden to me. I knew in my youth on the farm in Iowa that I wanted to be right where I am today, in the heart of the city.

I don't see the sky full of stars very often anymore like I did as a teenager sitting in my Rambler listening to WLS radio in Iowa. But the cars are still booming that bass beat through subwoofers, rattling the windows of my little apartment on the west side of Chicago. I am at home in the city.

Eat Your Vegetables—Children Are Starving

It was early on a Tuesday morning. I drove out to Wheaton College to be the main speaker at a breakfast for suburban pastors and ministry leaders. The topic they had given me was pretty broad. I was to talk about the poor.

We were experiencing our typical wintry Chicago weather, which included blowing snow and frigid temperatures. As I drove through the storm, I reflected on my message. I wanted to get beyond the guilt and paralysis, beyond the statistics about poverty and our dutiful responsibility to help the poor, to a deeper look at Scripture. I wanted to tell stories about how I had been blessed by the poor and how engaging with the poor would bring meaning to their lives.

I found my way through the snow to the

> *I won't cry any tears I'll just*
> *live without fear*
> *I'm so happy 'cause I'm living my*
> *life and I don't think about it.*
>
> —Emily Osment[1]

dining room that had been set with tables and chairs for the one hundred or so leaders that normally filled the room. As the time came to start the program, it was embarrassingly clear that attendance was down. Thirty or forty diehard attendees ate their eggs and bacon somberly.

The emcee apologized for the small size of the group, blaming the weather. I couldn't help but speculate on other overarching reasons for the low attendance. Who would want to get up early and travel through blustering snow to listen to someone talk about the depressing topic of the poor? Admittedly, trying to sort out how to relate to people who are poor can be downright depressing.

After all, haven't we been taken advantage of by cons on the street looking to make an easy buck by telling us some wild story?

Getting Duped

I recall when Ron came into our church office. He told me he needed money to get to work. He had a car, but it was out of gas, and he needed to get to Niles, a nearby suburb, to work at a nursing home. He told me the name of the nursing home and promised that when he got paid on Friday he would bring the money back to us. It sounded like a legitimate request. He wasn't asking for a handout, just a loan that he assured me he would pay back in full on payday.

On a hunch I called the nursing home. I was not surprised to hear they had never heard of Ron. He was not an employee there. I found out later that Ron was working the circuit of churches in the neighborhood, telling everyone his believable story. He was a con man.

Then there was Fred. Fred was upset because he was unable to give his daughter the fifteen dollars she needed to go on a school outing. He was homeless and didn't have the money. Could we please give him fifteen dollars so his daughter would not be excluded from the trip? My heart broke as I listened to his grief over his inability to provide for his young daughter. I was about to hand over the cash when I decided to call the school to ask about his daughter and the trip they were taking. Again, I was disappointed to discover that the school had no record of a student by the name he gave me. Fred hustled out the door.

A pastor I know who attended a local minister's group told his fellow ministers a shocking story of a man who came to him and swore him to secrecy. The man had told him a troubling but believable story about an act of violence he had committed. He was honest about it and repentant and won over the pastor's heart. Unfortunately, this man's life was now in danger. He was being followed by someone who was threatening to kill him. He desperately needed bus fare to get out of town. The story was so believable that the pastor gave him one hundred dollars for bus fare.

As the pastor told his story, two other ministers in the room groaned in disbelief. They, too, had given this masterful con man one hundred dollars.

There are classic con stories. Someone standing by a car flags you down with a gas can in tow and tells you he has run out of gas. He had a gas can, but it is empty. Can you just give him five dollars so he can buy enough gas to get home? You give him the money and drive by an hour later to find him still flagging down drivers.

Or someone comes out of a bathroom of a restaurant and tells the cashier he found a necklace on the floor. At that moment the restaurant gets a call from a collaborator who says he left the restaurant half an hour ago and is sure he lost the expensive necklace he had purchased for his wife's birthday in the bathroom. He is desperate to get the necklace back and offers a two-hundred-dollar reward. The one who discovered the lost article is delighted about the reward, but has to run to get to work. He agrees to leave the valuable necklace with the unsuspecting cashier and to split the reward with him. The cashier happily hands over one hundred dollars to the thief, thinking he will be reimbursed with the impending reward and is left with a dollar store necklace and no reward.

Many of the street scams are related to drug use. Desperate addicts will sell anything to get their next fix. They will strip the plumbing and copper wiring from their mother's apartment to sell it to recyclers. They will take food and clothing from homeless shelters and food pantries and sell it on the street for drugs. They will barter food stamps (or in Chicago, their Link card purchases) for cash. They will lie and steal. Anything to get enough cash for just one more hit.

I received an irate letter from a woman who told me to please take her off our Breakthrough mailing list. She didn't want to have anything to do with homeless people, because she had taken a homeless woman into her home, and the woman had left with pillowcases full of her stuff.

None of us enjoys knowing we have been duped. After experiencing two or three of these unfortunate confrontations, it is understandable that some would rather just avoid dealing with people in need. After all, aren't there government programs that take care of the legitimately poor and the unemployed? Why should we be bothered and chance contributing to someone's addiction or being taken advantage of again?

"I'm afraid to get too involved with people who have such desperate needs," Toni told me. "I know that if I get personally involved, it's going to get messy. I had an experience once where I was taken advantage of. A woman who was employed by me to clean our home came to me very upset that her parents were dying in the Philippines, and she needed money right away. I wrote her a check for several thousand dollars, and I never heard from her again. I felt like an idiot. I was angry. That's what I get scared of, that I'm just being foolish."

Feeling Overwhelmed

A student in one of my classes told us with tear-filled honesty that she was just plain tired of hearing about AIDS in Africa and seeing bloated bellies on TV. Even Oprah, *American Idol*, and Bono have gotten into the act, and it was simply too overwhelming. She said she felt paralyzed and was tired of feeling guilty all of the time.

"Eat those vegetables! Children are starving in Ethiopia!" my parents told me as a child, as if my little acts of dutiful responsibility would somehow solve the problem of world hunger. The notion of people starving in a faraway country was held over our heads like a club to instill gratitude for what we had and to remind us that many people throughout the world did not have enough.

The problems of the poor in our city and throughout the world can seem overwhelming. Even if we feel compassion and want to do something about poverty, we often don't know what to do. We feel small and insignificant in the face of such a mammoth task. How can I as an individual do anything to make a significant impact? Their real needs are just too complex. Checking out the requests people make can take a lot of time. Sometimes it seems easier just to give them the money to get rid of them.

Carrying Guilt

At one of my speaking engagements in which I urged Christians to adopt a lifestyle of compassion, a woman approached me, obviously moved by my message. "I make a lot of money," she said. "I feel guilty. I want to help, but I just don't know how. My job keeps me very busy and I don't have much time to volunteer. What should I do?"

I assured her that she didn't need to leave her high-paying job to engage with the poor. In fact, I believe strongly that God gives certain people the ability to create wealth. I will talk more about this in chapter 9. Investing her wealth to open doors of opportunity for struggling ministries among the poor could be the calling God has placed on her life.

Her friend, Susan, added, "I'm afraid I will lose my boundaries and give them everything for the wrong reasons. I start feeling guilty, and a sense of obligation comes over me, the sense that I've been so blessed, and it's my duty to do something to help. I tend to over give to compensate for the guilt I feel."

We feel guilty if we don't help and guilty if we do. There is plenty in life to feel guilty and depressed about without adding the weight of the world's desperate underclass on our shoulders.

Most of us whose worldviews have been shaped by Judeo-Christian values have some sense that we ought to be helping those less fortunate than ourselves. Many of us live with some uncomfortable guilt or at least reservation that we aren't doing enough. We may have read Ron Sider's *Rich Christians in an Age of Hunger* (or similar books) without ever having figured out how to respond.

Others of us may be very proud of how we have downsized our lifestyle and have taken the adage "Live simply so that others may simply live" to dramatic extremes. I know of one couple who got rid of their car and TV and have made the choice to live in a tiny apartment and dumpster dive for food. Another couple divested themselves of all electrical appliances. These people are making radical changes in their lifestyles, but are they really helping poor people?

I think most of us who are serious about following Christ really want to do the right thing. We may feel nagging guilt that we are not sacrificing enough, that somehow, there is something we are supposed to do, but we simply don't know what that is. We may even feel trapped in our own abundance, not sure of how to live in light of the privileges we have. We don't see our place for working in God's kingdom. We need practical solutions about how we should live our lives.

Out of a sense of guilt and obligation, we might take up special offerings for the poor, organize mission trips to Mexico or Haiti, or drop off sandwiches and blankets to shelters or areas in our city where the homeless congregate, and, for awhile, we feel better. It assuages our guilt and raises our consciousness about the fact that we have a lot; a lot of people don't have much; God loves the poor; and we should too.

We try to do our part to care for the needy, yet we are left wondering: Is that enough? Is God pleased? Will anything we do really make a difference anyway? Why should we even bother?

Why Bother?

It is actually easy to avoid thinking about the poor. Most of us who are wealthy or middle class in America don't need to make a conscious choice to avoid dealing with issues of poverty. We have already isolated ourselves from the poor by other choices—choices about where we live and shop and what schools we attend.

Apart from the somewhat startling stories of violence and shootings we see on the evening news, we can generally avoid seeing or thinking about the poor. We are not intentionally trying to isolate ourselves from the pain of the poor; we are simply living our lives in comfortable association with our family and friends in safe places where we are not bothered by the perplexing challenges of poverty.

In the Beatitudes of Jesus' Sermon on the Mount, captured in Matthew 5 and Luke 6, Jesus made the claim that the poor and the poor in spirit are blessed. What could he possibly have meant by that? If the poor are indeed blessed, it is one of our society's best kept secrets. Can you imagine a commercial on TV with a plainly dressed young woman waiting at a bus stop in a blizzard with the ad pitch being something like, "Finally, I found true happiness, taking the bus to work every day instead of that gas-guzzling Lexus SUV! Buy your bus card today and be free!" Downward economic mobility is not appealing to most of us.

Indeed, America was founded on the premise that we have the right to pursue our own happiness. It's the American dream to own a big, beautiful house. We can bypass impoverished sections of the city on the way to plays and ballgames, cruising on nicely landscaped causeways untarnished by the trash below.

Living the Abundant Life

I grew up in the baby boomer generation of America. My spirituality was formed in an era of incredible economic growth that led to unbridled consumerism. Parents of boomers lived through the Depression and two world wars, and they wanted their postwar babies to have a better life. So they doted over us. The economy was booming, industry was thriving, and we were handed what we came to believe we deserved: the good life.

As a generation, we began to accumulate more and more stuff like bigger houses, more cars, and more expensive TVs and electronic devices. We began to demand more travel, better hotels, water parks, and comfortable beds and chairs. Even the sizes of our meals and our waistlines expanded.

I know now that this economic growth and prosperity was not the experience of most others throughout the world, but I grew up unaware and unconcerned about systemic racism, economic injustice, and poverty. Those issues just didn't touch my life.

My worldview and my theology were shaped by individualism. Jesus came into the world to die for *me*. We were even taught to change the wording of John 3:16: "For God so loved *Arloa*, that he gave his only begotten son . . . that *Arloa* might not perish." Jesus died for me. If I was the only person in the world, Jesus would still have died for *me*.

While understanding and embracing the personal love of God for me and you is certainly important, my generation, for the most part, emphasized our personal walk with God to the exclusion of any notion of social concern or responsibility. What mattered most was whether I was right with God, and my highest concern for you was whether you were right with God. We weren't overly concerned with righteousness in our relationships with one another or whether we as a group of people might be unrighteous in the way our lives inadvertently oppressed other groups of people.

We often quoted John 10:10: "I have come that [you] might have life, and that [you] might have it more abundantly" (KJV). We embraced that in a very materialistic way as we accumulated lots of things. We equated prosperity with the blessing of God. Having lots of stuff was an indicator of God's blessing in our lives. I am blessed because I have things.

Did Jesus really say the poor are blessed, or just the poor in spirit? Matthew and Luke probably heard the same words from Jesus' mouth. Luke quotes Jesus as saying, "Blessed are the poor," while Matthew adds the words, "in spirit." Regardless, it makes sense that Jesus is implying that we all have something to learn from the experience of poverty, whether physically or spiritually. We may have found it convenient to spiritualize the words of Jesus rather than face poverty in our own lives and the lives of others.

We might even avoid dealing with the poor by judging them. Why don't they just get a job and pull themselves up by their bootstraps? Perhaps they are just lazy. Didn't Paul warn Timothy about not being taken advantage of by widows who are in the "habit of being idle and going about from house to house," those who were "gossips and busybodies" (1 Tim. 5:13)? The apostle Paul issued a very clear rule: "If a man will not work, he shall not eat" (2 Thess. 3:10).

Is there a group of people who could be categorized as the undeserving poor? If so, who are they? The able bodied who don't work? What if they want to work and can't find a job? What if the manufacturing jobs have been replaced by high tech jobs that necessitate a good education in a community where schools are failing? Are they the undeserving poor?

Of course there are lazy people, but before we decide that everyone who doesn't take advantage of opportunity is lazy, perhaps we need to know a little more about them. They may be experiencing a poverty of hope. In impoverished urban communities, where opportunities for economic advancement are rare, many just give up, assuming they will never be able to draw a legitimate income. That may look at first like laziness, but it is much more complex.

Who Are the Wealthy?

Clearly, economic poverty is relative. A family living on twenty thousand dollars per year in Bolivia may be quite comfortable, while a family of four in the United States would be living in poverty, and the family would be in crisis if they lived in Europe. When I traveled to Addis Ababa, Ethiopia, in 2005, I was amazed to learn that forty dollars per month was considered a pretty good salary for teachers there. Imagine what we can do with our financial gifts to support grassroots organizations in developing countries. I know individuals who live on a relatively moderate income in the U.S. who have built schools, clinics, and orphanages with just one gift.

While you may not consider yourself to be financially rich, I am going to assume, in a world in which half the population lives on less than two dollars per day, that most of you reading this book are extremely wealthy. A Web site, www.globalrichlist.com, will tabulate your income relative to the rest of the world. A salary of fifty thousand dollars will put you in the top 1 percent of the world's wealthiest. Unless your income is significantly less than that, you can be pretty sure that nearly 99 percent of the world's population is poorer than you.

As wealthy Christians in America, what is our responsibility toward the poor? Is there a better way than guilt and obligation? Can we really experience the blessing of God by being engaged with the poor? Can we learn about our own poverty from those who know their reliance on God for their very survival? Can we be blessed by understanding our own poverty and need for God?

Experiencing God

Henry Blackaby wrote in his book *Experiencing God*, "If God shows you where He is working, immediately join Him!"[2] I have found God to be visibly present and powerfully at work in the inner city of Chicago and in other impoverished communities throughout the world. It is in those places that I have most profoundly experienced God.

Psalm 34:18 says that God "is close to the brokenhearted." Perhaps when we come alongside the brokenhearted, we get near God, too. At least that seems consistent with the astounding claim Jesus made in Matthew 25 that when we feed the hungry, give drink to the thirsty, clothe people, take in strangers, care for the sick, and visit those who are in prison we are actually ministering to him. "I tell you the truth, whatever you did for one of the least of these brothers of mine, you did for me" (Matt. 25:40). It makes sense, then, that these practices would be central to what it means to be a Christian, a lover and follower of Jesus.

I experienced my own epiphany of ministering to Jesus when Charles came to Breakthrough. He was obviously in great pain. He complained that his feet hurt. He was an elderly man who had difficulty reaching down to care for his feet. He had been walking all night to stay warm and was exhausted. I knelt down and gingerly removed his worn-out shoes from his feet and then his crusty socks. His feet were cracked and bleeding and gave off an obnoxious odor.

I got a dishpan and filled it with warm soapy water. We soaked his feet in the warm water for nearly an hour. Then I took his feet in my hands. I dried them with a soft towel and rubbed lotion on them.

Suddenly it was as if the whole present reality of what I was doing in the physical world gave way to the profound realization that Jesus had asked us to do this very thing—to wash one another's feet—and what I was doing for this lonely, old man, I was, in a sense, doing to Jesus himself. I felt such awe and joy and intimacy with Jesus at that moment.

Mother Teresa said we meet Jesus "in his distressing disguise" as we care for the poor and needy. So it was that in the midst of a very ordinary act of love, I also experienced Jesus.

Thus this journey to the poor is an invitation, an invitation to know God in a deeper and more meaningful way, an invitation to be near God and to experience God more profoundly, an invitation to grow in your love for Jesus and for those he loves.

The poor are not a burden. We don't need to feel guilty about what we have or whether we are doing enough. We don't need to judge or worry about being taken advantage of. We don't have to feel overwhelmed by the perplexity of the issues. Instead, we can learn to love all people with the same love we have received and in doing so find the gateway to the kingdom. "For theirs is the kingdom of heaven," said Jesus (Matt. 5:3), and he invites us to enter the joy of kingdom life.

I was moved by the words of one of my favorite preachers, the rock star Bono, at the NAACP Awards Ceremony in 2007:

True religion will not let us fall asleep in the comfort of our freedom. Love thy neighbor is not a piece of advice, it's a command. That means that in the global village we're going to have to start loving a whole lot more people.

Because where you live should not determine whether you live or whether you die.

And to those in the church who still sit in judgment on the AIDS emergency, let me climb into the pulpit for just one moment. Because whatever thoughts we have about God, who he is, or even if God exists, most will agree, that God has a special place for the poor. The poor are where God lives. God is in the slums, in the cardboard boxes where the poor play house.

God is where the opportunity is lost and lives are shattered. God is with the mother who has infected her child with a virus that will take both their lives. God is under the rubble in the cries we hear during war time. God, my friend, is with the poor. And God is with us if we are with them.

This is not a burden. This is an adventure. Don't let anyone tell you it cannot be done. We can be the generation that ends extreme poverty.[3]

3

You Will Always Have the Poor with You

I was being interviewed by my friend Anita Lustrea on her award-winning radio show when a woman called in and asked a question I hear often from well-meaning Christians: "Didn't even Jesus say in Matthew 26:11 that we would always have the poor with us?"

I felt I knew what she was getting at. If even Jesus acknowledged we would always be surrounded by poor people, didn't that kind of let us off the hook? Wasn't that reason enough to acknowledge there is really nothing we can do to fundamentally change the plight of the poor? We might help an isolated person here or there temporarily; but if poverty is inevitable,

> God sees our community primarily as an exhibition, not a laboratory. Our Spirit-drenched oneness is the most important way His spectacularness is displayed on earth. . . . Never does the world see Christ more clearly than when His love flows freely among believers.
>
> —Dwight Edwards

why bother? We can drive by and drop off sandwiches to show our compassion or deposit a dollar or two in someone's outstretched cup, but certainly our little gestures will never really change anything. Even Jesus acknowledged that!

Resignation

Did Jesus mean that poverty is something we should tolerate because it is just the way things are? He was, after all, referring to Deuteronomy 15:11: "There will always be poor people in the land." Is poverty, then, so inevitable that there's nothing we can really do to change it?

What many of us don't realize is the context for that quote. Deuteronomy 15:4–5 says, "There should be no poor among you, for in the land the LORD your God is giving you to possess as your inheritance, he will richly bless you, if only you fully obey the LORD your God and are careful to follow all these commands I am giving you today." What were those commands? They included a set of instructions for aiding those in need, the periodic cancellation of debts, and the practice of generous giving when resources get out of balance. The passage goes on to say, "If anyone is poor among your people in any of the towns of the land that the LORD your God is giving you, do not be hardhearted or tightfisted toward them. Rather, be openhanded and freely lend them whatever they need" (vv. 7–8 TNIV).

It was the failure to obey these commands that led to the condition of perpetual poverty Jesus identified. As long as they lived in disobedience, they would have the poor among them.

How dramatic was the contrast of Jesus' followers in the early church, of whom it was said, "There were no needy persons among them" (Acts 4:34).

The Invisible

Jesus was right; there will always be someone who needs our help, but ongoing, systemic poverty results from failure to help, our failure to obey God. Sin distorts relationships and poverty results. Jesus was not excusing us from involvement with the poor. He was reminding us that poverty is an indicator that we have missed something central to the heart and intention of God. Poverty is not God's design. It's not the way things are supposed to be.

The teachings of the Law laid out many practices to protect the poor. Naomi's daughter-in-law Ruth was able work meaningfully by "glean[ing] in the fields behind the harvesters" (Ruth 2:3), rather than being reduced to begging. This was a common practice that was instituted by God, who had instructed them, "When you reap the harvest of your land, do not reap to the very edges of your field or gather the gleanings of your harvest. Leave them for the poor and the alien. I am the LORD your God" (Lev. 23:22). Boaz, who later became Ruth's husband, was a kind man who took the command even further. He instructed his workers, "Pull out some stalks for her from the bundles and leave them for her to pick up" (Ruth 2:16). He told them to leave stalks for her on purpose.

God instructed landowners to let their land lie dormant every seventh year so the poor would have food. Like Ruth, the poor would still have to work to gather what they needed, but they were to be given opportunity. "But during the seventh year let the land lie unplowed and unused. Then the poor among your people may get food from it, and the wild animals may eat what they leave. Do the same with your vineyard and your olive grove" (Ex. 23:11).

At the end of three years, they were to "bring all the tithes of that year's produce and store it in your towns, so that the Levites (who have no allotment or inheritance of their own) and the aliens, the fatherless and the widows who live in your towns may come and eat and be satisfied" (Deut. 14:28–29).

The Lord told Moses on Mount Sinai that every fiftieth year was to be declared a Year of Jubilee in which slaves would be set free, debts cancelled, and land returned to its original owner (Lev. 25:8–55). Jesus alluded to this Jubilee year when he declared in Luke 4:18–19 that he had come to bring good news to the poor, freedom to prisoners, sight to the blind, release for the oppressed, and to proclaim the year of the Lord's favor.

God did not prevent those who had acquired land from prospering from their acquisitions; nor did he require them to give back all the wealth they had accumulated from their good fortune or hard work. What God did require, however, was that they return the additional land they had acquired to its original owner so that the next generation could have the opportunity for prosperity it represented.

This returning of the land affirmed that all belonged to God (Lev. 25:23) and assured that no generation would be without opportunity because of the previous generation's poor management or unfortunate circumstances that may have caused them to lose their land. Each new generation was given a chance to be who God made them to be.

In a day when so much wealth and power are in the hands of so few and so many people have no real opportunity at prosperity, it is especially important to consider God's heart on this matter. We have a responsibility to speak against any systemic injustice which robs a person of a real chance at a better life. If people have stewarded the opportunities and blessings they have been given in a way that has prospered them, that is a good thing. But they must not ignore the plight of those who, generation after generation, have been denied such opportunity. This matters to God.

God's commands in Deuteronomy are clear. Our response to the poor is to be openhanded. Moreover, we are to enjoy sharing what God has given us. "Give generously to [the poor] and do so without a grudging heart." The result of this attitude of sharing is that the "LORD your God will bless you in all your work and in everything you put your hand to" (Deut. 15:10). Giving to the poor will not diminish us. It releases a flow from the heart of God to us and through us to others that will never be depleted.

Selective Focus on Scripture

Those of us who are boomers, who grew up in the evangelical Christian church in the fifties and sixties, didn't hear much about the more than two thousand verses in Scripture about the poor.[1] In fact, many of us were taught a theology that ignored or spiritualized away many of the references to the poor in Scripture.

Since my childhood, I have attended churches that honored the authority and relevance of Scripture to guide daily life. But it has been my experience that Christian churches in communities that are relatively untouched by issues of poverty tend to ignore large portions of the Bible that speak into difficult social issues.

It is understandable that pastors and teachers prepare messages that will relate to the lives of the people in their congregations. They contextualize Scripture by the passages they choose to teach and the applications they make. As ministers prepare sermons to meet the needs of people in racially and economically segregated congregations, quite different theological frameworks emerge.

The following chart compares the differences in the core issues addressed in the town of George, Iowa, where I grew up, and messages I hear in East Garfield Park, the impoverished community in Chicago where I now live. The theology developed in churches in geographical areas that are relatively untouched by issues of poverty tend to emphasize the personal implications of the gospel, while those in impoverished communities emphasize God's intervention in the social needs of people.

Contextualized

George	East Garfield
• Individual responsibility	• Social justice
• Economic independence	• Survival
• Personal piety	• Racism/oppression
• Family	• Basic human needs
• Success	• Suffering
• Leisure time	• Empowerment

When we live in isolated communities, our theology is shaped, in part, by our context. To get a whole theology, we need to understand how Scripture would be applied in other contexts. If we don't, our theology is myopic and truncated, and we might actually miss some very important themes from Scripture, or interpret them in ways that work for us, but not necessarily for the rest of the world.

When I began attending urban churches, I was surprised by their focus on passages I had rarely heard before, passages that spoke of the exodus of the Israelites from slavery, passages that related to suffering and overcoming pain and sorrow, passages that promised the provision of God in the midst of great need, passages that spoke of justice and empowerment for the children of God.

I studied the story of the exodus in Sunday school, but it hadn't been preached as an inspiration for enduring and seeking God's deliverance from oppression and injustice. That was because most of the people in my farming community of George, Iowa, didn't face those problems.

I began to realize that much of the printed literature—the books and magazines and Sunday school materials—from which I had learned about God—were primarily written in contexts where care for the poor was only a distant concern, a Thanksgiving benevolence offering, or a Christmas used-clothing drive. Not a central focus.

One Sunday morning, I was privileged to bring the Scripture meditation on Women's Day at the New Landmark Missionary Baptist Church. I got to sit in the pulpit (that is, on the platform) beside Rev. Cy Field's wife, Yolanda, who serves as Breakthrough's director of adult services. I loved the Litany for Women, which was read responsively. It was so unlike anything I have ever heard in my church background.

All knowing God, who sees and helps to bear the pains and disappointments of every black mother, we ask that you extend to our mothers comfort and strength.

We pray for women everywhere. They give us life and love and hold our families together. Amid changing family structures, we remember mothers young and old, single mothers and fathers, homeless mothers, grandmothers, godmothers, and surrogate mothers.

We pray for women who suffer due to unemployment, insufficient housing, and poor healthcare. Heal black mothers, Lord, as they have often experienced mistreatment and witnessed the harsh abuse of their children, husbands, siblings, and parents.

Awesome Savior, fortify our sisters. Continue to make for them a refuge in the time of trouble.

We pray for mothers and their children, as violent crimes and drug abuse conspire to tear the fiber of black families.

We pray for women of old who have bent their backs cleaning homes, picking cotton, and working by the sweat of their brow. We thank them for their determination and their belief that education is a door to liberation and success.

God, empower women to enrich the lives of their families. Aid them as they teach sons and daughters determination and the value of investing in the future.

Women have always been activists and leaders, teaching us how to live and making our communities better. We remember poet and writer Frances E. W. Harper, who birthed a crusade against lynching during Reconstruction.

We remember Rosa Parks who birthed a bus boycott and Shirley Chisholm who blazed the trail to high public office for black women.

We cherish sisters who teach, write, or preach the truth and who open the minds of children to limitless possibility. We celebrate women who are homemakers, educators, authors, and pastors who formulate ideas, expend creative energy, and inspire young people to become leaders.

They have been a loving presence in business, in play, in the arts, and in all of life.

Because women taught us that "the Lord will make a way out of no way," we have the inheritance of a powerful spiritual legacy. We give women bouquets of gratitude and honor. Kind and gentle Savior, ever bless them.

What We Missed

My friend Cindy recently read through the Bible and highlighted every passage that referred to justice and care for the poor. "Do you know what Solomon asked God for?" she asked me.

"Sure," I replied, confident in my Sunday school education. "He asked God for wisdom, and God gave him the bonus of riches and honor."

She looked at me with a triumphant gotcha gleam. "Close, but I read the first few chapters of 1 Kings this morning. Guess what? Solomon asked God to give "your servant a discerning heart to govern your people and to distinguish between right and wrong . . . discernment in *administering justice*" (1 Kings 3:9–13, emphasis added).

Cindy grinned at me. "I've always believed Solomon asked for wisdom, which is true, but his wisdom would have been a mere ego trip had it not been tied to administering justice. That's what pleased the Lord enough to give him the bonuses of riches and honor.

"Later, when Scripture records his wise judgment between the two women fighting over the baby, the Bible says all Israel feared the king 'because they saw that he had wisdom from God to administer *justice*'" (1 Kings 3:28, emphasis added).

It seemed so clear. How had I missed that?

We hear the verses extolling the virtuous woman in Proverbs 31 (beginning with v. 10) nearly every Mothers' Day. She worked hard, rising early to care for her family. But we rarely hear the verses just before them. Verses 8 and 9 say, "Speak up for those who cannot speak for themselves, for the rights of all who are destitute. Speak up and judge fairly; defend the rights of the poor and needy."

Concerned that we might confuse faith and righteousness for works and righteousness, we memorized Ephesians 2:8–9, stressing that we are not saved by our good works, but we ignored the next verse that says, "For we are God's workmanship, created in Christ Jesus to do good works, which God prepared in advance for us to do." We missed the purposeful outcome of saving faith, thinking it ensured only a distant future in heaven but missing that we were saved to serve, to join with Jesus in the re-creation of a just and loving world.

Jesus' mother proclaimed that Jesus would lift up the humble and fill the hungry with good things (Luke 1:52–53). She knew the messianic

Rhonda

Rhonda's parents died when she was nine, so she went to live with her grandmother. Her grandmother was a church-going woman and took Rhonda to church several times each week. What Gramma didn't know was that Rhonda was being repeatedly raped by a deacon at the church in the choir robe closet. Rhonda soon learned to escape immediately out the backdoor of the church before the deacon could catch her. She felt it was safer on the streets than in the church.

It wasn't long before Rhonda was using heroin and selling her body on the street in order to buy her next fix. Rhonda survived a thirty-year heroin addiction and contracted HIV in the process. One night, she met Brenda who was ministering on the street with Breakthrough's outreach RV. Brenda pursued a relationship with Rhonda for nearly eight years, visiting her in jails, hospitals, and rehab centers, praying with her and taking her to church.

Eventually Rhonda's addiction got the best of her, and her weight dwindled to a frail sixty pounds. The nursing home doctor told her to prepare herself because she was dying. Finally, in desperation, Rhonda cried out to the Lord, "God, if you are not going to take me home, I would at least like to walk."

Miraculously, God set Rhonda free from her addiction, and within weeks, she was walking. She steadily regained her health and put on weight. Today Rhonda is active in a local church and has started a ministry to reach out to other women on the street who are struggling with HIV and AIDS.

kingdom would flip her social world upside down. The rich, mighty, and proud in Jerusalem would be sent away. Poor farmers and shepherds would be exalted and honored. Her song was a song of hope for the underclass. Jesus was coming to make all things right, to bring a new way of justice and peace.

John the Baptist announced the coming of the Messiah by quoting from Isaiah 40 and proclaiming, "A voice of one calling in the desert, 'Prepare the way for the Lord, make straight paths for him. Every valley shall be filled in, every mountain and hill made low. The crooked roads shall become straight, the rough ways smooth. And all mankind will see God's salvation'" (Luke 3:4–6). John's dramatic description portrays a revolutionary new kingdom: full valleys, flat mountains, straight curves, and level bumps. John warns us that in Christ, the playing field would be leveled. Jesus would bring an end to the steep and rocky road of the oppressed.

Jesus' teaching about the sheep and the goats in Matthew 25 actually seems to indicate that the way we treat "the least of these" is a pretty good indicator of where we will spend eternity (Matt. 25:45–46). True followers of Christ would be recognized by their efforts to provide food, water, and clothing for the needy and by looking after those sick and in prison. Those who love Jesus would love the ones Jesus loves, the world he came to die for. Christians would be known by their love for the poor, the despised, the social outcasts.

We missed the significance of the overarching story of Jesus, that though he was God, he did not cling to his power, but relinquished it, coming to earth as a vulnerable, naked, utterly helpless baby. He grew up in a working-class family and would say as an adult that he had "no place to lay his head" (Matt. 8:20). He learned through suffering.

Jesus modeled self-sacrificing love for the poor. The apostle Paul wrote, "For you know the grace of our Lord Jesus Christ, that though he was rich, yet for your sakes he became poor, so that you through his poverty might become rich" (2 Cor. 8:9).

He crossed boundaries of race, class, and gender with the woman at the well. He actually let a prostitute wipe his feet with her hair in an act of tender love for him. He illustrated what was most important to God by telling the story of a despised Samaritan man who went out of his way to care for a Jewish man who had been beaten, robbed, and left to die (Luke 10:30–37).

He proclaimed that the first would be last and the last first; the least would be greatest; those who lose their lives would find them; and the worst sinners would experience the greatest love. He taught us to seek the lowest position, take the backseat, be like a child, and follow him in service because, as he said, "I am among you as one who serves" (Luke 22:27). He modeled loving service by taking a basin and a towel to wash his disciples' dirty feet.

Though the ultimate purpose in Jesus' crucifixion was not merely to establish solidarity with the poor and other outcasts, he nevertheless was "despised and rejected . . . Like one from whom people hide their faces . . . we held him in low esteem" (Isa. 53:3 TNIV). He experienced extreme psychological and spiritual anguish in the garden of Gethsemane as he sweat drops of blood under the pressure of what he knew lay ahead. He was betrayed by Judas, one of his chosen followers and denied by one of his best friends, Peter. Though innocent, he was whipped and tormented, spit upon and ridiculed by civic and religious leaders and an angry mob. He carried his heavy cross throughout the narrow, rocky streets of Jerusalem, and he died an excruciatingly painful death on the cross, abandoned even by God the Father.

In agony on the cross, Jesus cried out in distress, "My God, my God, why have you forsaken me?" (Matt. 27:46).

Jesus understands our need to ask why. Why, God? Why do the poor suffer so? Who's to blame? Why are they denied access to proper healthcare and a quality education? Why are they tormented and ridiculed? Why are they hungry and thirsty?

Scripture sheds some light on the why questions of poverty by addressing issues of greed, disobedience, isolation, discrimination, and the breakdown of the world as it was meant to be. But ultimately the power to overcome poverty lies not so much in assigning blame, as in learning to live the Jesus way, to follow him in how he interacted with the poor and the marginalized, and to be willing—like Jesus, to lay down our self-centered, materialistic lives to take up the cross of loving generosity, gentle kindness, and tenacious advocacy for the rights of the poor and the oppressed.

We don't know if the Father ever answered Jesus' why question, but we do know that Jesus understands the sorrow of the poor and of all those who suffer. Jesus knows what it is like to be scorned and ridiculed. Jesus understands deep agony. He let himself be crushed by the weight of the sin of the world on the cross, and he asks us to follow him by denying ourselves and taking up that cross every day.

The Christian life is a journey to the cross from which there is no turning back. It is about learning to lay down our lives for others because of love. Yes, we will always have the poor with us until someday when the kingdom comes in full and "sorrow and sighing will flee away" (Isa. 35:10). Therefore, we are to be openhanded and generous. "And do so without a grudging heart; then because of this the LORD your God will bless you in all your work and in everything you put your hand to" (Deut. 15:10).

As I have studied Scripture in an urban context, I have come to see how central justice and compassionate care for the poor are to the message of the "good news to the poor" that Jesus said he came to proclaim (Luke 4:18–19). To embrace the gospel means to embrace the message and mission of Christ. Our experience of salvation doesn't just affect our eternal destiny; it touches the way we live now on the earth.

Preaching *and* Living the Gospel

Throughout the ages, for millions of Christians, there never was any question that our task was to preach the gospel *and* serve the poor, the needy, and the oppressed. That is just how one lives the gospel. Consider these great heroes of the faith.

William and Catherine Booth, founders of the Salvation Army in 1865, preached the gospel *and* fed the hungry—thousands of them—and fought the tavern owners and gin dealers who oppressed the poor. Even political action came naturally. They staged seventeen days of nonstop protests in London and gathered three hundred ninety-three thousand signatures on a petition to Parliament, demanding the government pass and enforce laws against the rampant sex slave trade of young girls in a city said to have eighty thousand prostitutes.

Gladys Aylward, missionary to China during the 1930s, preached the gospel *and* became the Mandarin's official foot inspector to help bring an end to the grotesque practice of binding the feet of small girls to prevent their feet from growing.

David Livingstone, known as the great explorer-missionary to Africa, fought the slave trade wherever he encountered it. He forcibly freed captives from slave caravans and stirred up such an international protest that Britain revoked his royal commission during his third expedition, ordering him back to England. He did not obey, and later died in Africa on his own.

Amy Carmichael, missionary to India at the beginning of the twentieth century, spread the gospel *and* rescued hundreds of children from temple prostitution.

George Müller did not believe in asking people for money to carry out God's work. He prayed and God provided while his small congregation grew twelvefold in a few years. In 1835, he opened the first orphanage for poor children in England. His work grew into five large homes, where he ultimately cared for over ten thousand children during his lifetime—all through prayer and without soliciting funds.

Mary Slessor, pioneer missionary to Africa, believed school *and* the gospel went hand in hand. She had no reservations about challenging the establishment on such things as twin murder, human sacrifice, polygamy, and slavery.

Elizabeth Fry always found time to help the poor by providing warm clothes, medicine, and hot soup. But her faith in Christ motivated her to become the driving force behind new legislation to make the treatment of prisoners more humane in England in the first half of the nineteenth century.

In the name of Christ, **William Wilberforce** fought against slavery in England and ultimately won. But before that in 1791, **John Wesley**, the great preacher and founder of the Methodist movement, wrote to him: "If God is with you, who can be against you? Oh, be not weary in well-doing.

Go on, in the name of God and in the power of his might till even American slavery, the vilest that ever saw the sun, shall banish away before it."

In 1836, at the age of sixteen, **Florence Nightingale** wrote in her diary: "God spoke to me and called me to his service." She became the founder of modern nursing.

In the mid-nineteenth century, **Charles Loring Brace** was asked to head up the Children's Aid Society to care for the overwhelming number of orphans wandering the streets of New York City. He came up with the idea of arranging for their foster care by families in the expanding American West. Thus the orphan trains were born, and about two hundred thousand children found homes with families rather than in institutions or on city streets.

If there is anything to the claim that the United States was formed on Christian principles, then those founders who were true believers considered it not only their right but their duty to oppose the oppression and injustice they experienced from England, as the preamble to the U.S. Constitution states, "in Order to form a more perfect Union, establish Justice, insure domestic Tranquility, provide for the common defense, promote the general Welfare, and secure the Blessings of Liberty to ourselves and our Posterity."

How to Show Love to the Poor

The context in which Jesus said we would always have the poor among us is actually very beautiful. It was near the time of his death. There was already a buzz among the chief priests and the teachers of the law about how they were going to kill Jesus. Jesus was in Bethany at the home of Simon the Leper, reclining at the table, when a woman—a prostitute—entered with an alabaster jar full of expensive perfume.

It was common for a woman of the night to wear a small alabaster jar of perfume as a necklace. Since she couldn't shower often, she would dab on a bit of the perfume so she would smell good for her customers. The alabaster jar had a very narrow neck and a small opening so it wouldn't spill easily. It would have been impossible to pour out the perfume without breaking the jar. Awed by the gentle compassion of Jesus, and throwing caution to the wind, she broke the jar and poured out the perfume on Jesus' feet and wiped them off with her hair and tears.

This woman, a notorious public sinner, took her most precious commodity and poured it out at Jesus' feet in an act of loving adoration. The alabaster jar of perfume represented the very essence of who she was and whatever power she possessed. Jesus lovingly accepted her unbridled devotion as she broke the jar and lavishly poured it out on him.

Some who were present became indignant and rebuked her for wasting so much money on such an extravagant gesture. The perfume could have been sold for a year's wages, they argued, and given to the poor. Jesus came to her defense, saying, "The poor you will always have with you, and you can help them any time you want. But you will not always have me. She did what she could. She poured perfume on my body beforehand to prepare for my burial" (Mark 14:7–8).

I don't know exactly what all that means, but I can't help but think there is symbolism in what happened that goes far beyond our typical interpretation of this verse, which tries to excuse us from involvement with the poor.

Jesus would soon be gone from the earth physically, but he would live on symbolically in "the least of these": the poor, the misfits, and the rejected. Perhaps Jesus was commending this lavish outpouring of self-giving love as an example of the generous way we are to express our love for Jesus through our gifts to "the least of these"—to sacrifice any power we may have and lay it at Jesus' feet through our loving care for the poor.

Jesus is not here in bodily form, but the poor are still with us, and Jesus said we can love on them any time we want. How extravagant is our love? Are we willing to let ourselves be broken and spilled out as we pour lavish love on Jesus through our love for the poor? Jesus is not advocating a stingy outpouring of love but an extravagant, selfless one that gives our best.

Jesus honored the woman who poured the perfume on his head, because she "did what she could." That's what Jesus asks of us—to do what we can. How willing are you to pour out your love on Jesus through your love for the poor?

Broken and spilled out,
Just for love of you, Jesus,
My most precious treasure
Lavished on thee.
Broken and spilled out
And poured at your feet.
In sweet abandon
Let me be spilled out
And used up for thee.

—recorded by Steve Green[2]

Three Kinds of Churches

4

What if our churches are missing the heart of the gospel? What if we have ignored a significant part of the good news Jesus came to announce—particularly his concern for justice and compassion for the poor? Then how do we turn to embrace the whole message and mission of Christ?

In Acts 20:27, the apostle Paul told the elders from the church of Ephesus that he had not hesitated to proclaim to them the "whole counsel of God" (NKJV). Many church leaders are beginning to recognize that if they teach and preach only what's-in-it-for-me messages, they are missing much of the message of the gospel.

> Neither politicians nor philanthropists can offer people what they need the most—the incarnate love of Christ. Unless the Church fulfills its responsibility to proclaim by word and deed the "Good News to the poor," the poor have no true hope. We, the Church, bear the only true gospel of hope.
>
> —John Perkins

I have found it helpful to think of churches in three general categories. The first is the church that essentially ignores issues related to God's concern for the poor while focusing almost exclusively on personal evangelism and personal growth. I call it the *personal piety church.*

The second type of church recognizes compassion and justice as important and forms a compassion committee or social concerns ministry as one of the many ministries within the life of the church. While this group represents legitimate issues, those who participate are a small minority within the church and often feel they need to compete with the other ministries of the church for significance. I call it the *social justice committee church.*

I call the third type of church *compassionate to the core.* This is the church in which compassion, reconciliation, and justice are core values that permeate every aspect of church life.

To follow Jesus means not only that we love God, but that we follow the example of Jesus in loving and caring for people, especially those who are most broken and oppressed by society, the "least of these," as Jesus called them.

The Personal Piety Church

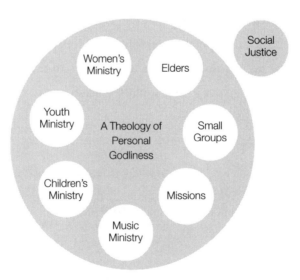

As I mentioned before, many churches tend to emphasize personal godliness to the exclusion of social justice. Some of the leaders of these churches are fearful that if they emphasize social issues, the church might cross a line into the dreaded territory of becoming a social gospel church.

As we saw in the last chapter, this fear is not only foreign to the gospel of Jesus, but it never crossed the minds of most of the heroes of the faith down through the ages who both preached *and* lived the gospel.

So how and when did this fear arise? The fear has deep roots in a reaction formed in fundamentalist churches in the 1930s and 1940s to the teaching of Walter Rauschenbusch. Rauschenbusch, a professor of church history at Rochester Seminary in New York, came face-to-face with oppressive poverty during his twelve-year pastorate in a Baptist church in the city.[1] He became disillusioned with capitalism and began to advocate for a kind of communism or Christian socialism.

Fundamentalists condemned his teaching when he claimed that "the essential purpose of Christianity" was to "transform human society into the kingdom of God by regenerating all human relationships."[2] He identified the kingdom of God with "a reconstruction of society on a Christian basis"[3] and implied that human beings can establish the divine kingdom by themselves (whereas Jesus spoke of it as a gift of God). Evangelicals were understandably concerned about this politicization of the kingdom and concentrated on personal evangelism, steering away from sociopolitical action.

Another factor contributing to the neglect of social concern among fundamentalists was the teaching of J. N. Darby and the popularization of the Scofield Bible and premillennialism. *The Scofield Study Bible* sold three million copies in fifty years, helping make Darby's prophetic beliefs the norm for English-speaking evangelicals.[4]

Darby's teaching:

> portrays the present evil world as beyond improvement or redemp-
> tion, and predicts instead that it will deteriorate steadily until the
> coming of Jesus, who will then set up his millennial reign on earth. If
> the world is getting worse, and if only Jesus at his coming will put it
> right, the argument runs, there seems no point in trying to reform it.
> Adopting social programs is "like cleaning the staterooms on the
> Titanic after it hit the iceberg. . . . It is far more important simply to
> preach the Gospel and to rescue souls for the next life."[5]

The shift is demonstrated in D. L. Moody's writings. Moody helped
to found the YMCA and was involved in charitable endeavors in the
city, demonstrating that social involvement and evangelism naturally go
together. Eventually, however, Moody was drawn away from social
action as intrinsic to the gospel and into the Scofield-Darby movement
that emphasized eternal destiny to the exclusion of present participation
in caring for physical needs of "the least of these." Moody wrote:

> When I was at work for the City Relief Society before the fire I
> used to go to a poor sinner with the Bible in one hand and a loaf of
> bread in the other . . . My idea was that I could open a poor man's
> heart by giving him a load of wood or a ton of coal when the winter
> was coming on, but I soon found out that he wasn't any more inter-
> ested in the Gospel on that account. Instead of thinking how he
> could come to Christ, he was thinking how long it would be before
> he got the load of wood. If I had the Bible in one hand and a loaf in
> the other the people always looked first at the loaf; and that was
> just the contrary of the order laid down in the Gospel.[6]

John Stott writes that another reason for the alienation of some churches from social concern in the early twentieth century was the spread of Christianity among the middle class, who tended to dilute it by identifying it with their own culture. Stott quotes a summary by David Moberg of the sociological findings reported by Milton Rokeach in 1969:

> The general picture that emerges . . . is that those who place a high value on salvation are conservative, anxious to maintain the status quo, and unsympathetic or indifferent to the plight of the black and the poor . . . Considered all together, the data suggest a portrait of the religious-minded as a person having a self-centered preoccupation with saving his own soul, an other-worldly orientation, coupled with indifference toward or even a tacit endorsement of a social system that would perpetuate social inequality and injustice.[7]

Carl Ellis emphasizes that justice and personal godliness are two sides of the same coin. The coin is the kingdom of God and his righteousness. He says:

> Sadly, many White evangelical, fundamentalist and Reformed churches . . . have been rendered dysfunctional by a defective view of theology and culture. They failed to distinguish between White standards and scriptural standards. Their theology had led them to a preoccupation with private salvation. Many leading evangelicals never came to grips with the big picture of God's purposes. They never saw the broad cultural implications of the Great Commission. This is why their Christianity never had application beyond the private aspects of life.[8]

The central error of this type of church is that it holds a truncated view of the gospel. When Jesus proclaimed in Luke 4 that he had come to bring good news to the poor, he went on to describe what that would entail. "He has sent me to proclaim freedom for the prisoners and recovery of sight for the blind, to release the oppressed, to proclaim the year of the Lord's favor" (Luke 4:18–19).

Receiving the good news is not just a personal affirmation of Jesus' substitutionary death on the cross and hope of life in heaven after death. Embracing the gospel of Jesus involves embracing a new way of life. Living out the gospel includes meeting physical needs of broken people, releasing them from their bondage and oppression, and bringing them into an experience of God's favor in this present life. Becoming a Christ follower is more than intellectual assent to the work of Christ on the cross; it is a decision to follow Jesus in the way of the cross, a way of sacrifice and love. The gospel is indeed very good news for the poor because it means love will not only flow to them from God, but through fellow Christ followers.

James addressed the personal piety type of church in the second chapter of his book when he wrote:

> What good is it, my brothers and sisters, if people claim to have faith but have no deeds? Can such faith save them? Suppose a brother or sister is without clothes and daily food. If one of you says to them, "Go in peace; keep warm and well fed," but does nothing about their physical needs, what good is it? In the same way, faith by itself, if it is not accompanied by action, is dead. (James 2:14–17 TNIV)

Therefore, faith that is not expressed in care for the poor is not true Christian faith.

Before I started Breakthrough, I had the erroneous notion that most people were on the street because they didn't have a personal relationship with Jesus. I stereotyped homeless people as rebellious wanderers whose lives would be transformed if they just received Christ. If we could hook them with coffee and good food, we might be able to win their souls, and that would change everything. They would be reconciled with their families, live in homes with white picket fences, and bring their children to Sunday school.

What I discovered was that many of the people who came to us already had deep faith in Christ. They had just become trapped in a social and economic system that kept them at the bottom. Certainly some did need to hear the good news that Jesus had died for their sins, but most seemed to know that already. They needed to experience the loving support of the faith community to help them get out of the pit in which they found themselves. The real sin that needed to be confronted was the social sin of oppression that had kept them locked in poverty.

The Social Justice Committee Church

Another approach some churches take is to include social justice as one of the many activities of the church. Congregants can choose from a menu of activities, and the social justice committee or the community care committee is one of many. It is available for those who choose the social justice committee like they would choose singing in the choir.

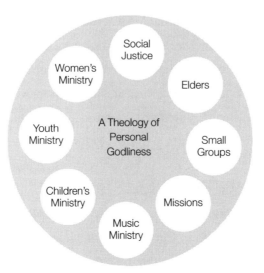

The social justice committee will occasionally sponsor service opportunities in which members of the church can participate. They may organize a prison ministry or a coat drive. They keep the church informed about opportunities to serve at shelters and soup kitchens. Often this is a small group of compassionate souls who feel they are carrying the burden for the church and are competing for time with the multiple meetings of the other church activities.

The worship in these churches tends to continue to be individualistic in nature, usually focusing on one's personal relationship with Jesus and the benefits that result. "I" pronouns rather than "we" are often used in the songs that are sung.

The Compassionate to the Core Church

This is the church in which the leadership has come to understand and embrace the centrality of God's heart for justice in their understanding of the good news of the gospel. Promoting both personal godliness and social justice is core to the church's mission, vision, and values. Leaders and members emphasize both in every aspect of church life. Spiritual disciplines include justice and compassion activities as well as personal Bible study and prayer. Righteous behavior is not restricted to such things as honesty, moderation, sexual purity, and faithfulness, but must also include hospitality, acts of charity, help for the poor, and advocacy for justice.

This model does not preclude the fact that Christ's church functions as a body with various members equipped for specialized tasks. What it requires, however, is that the whole body is going in the same direction, with the same purpose, goals, and passion. Churches that are compassionate to the core recognize that the gospel is indeed good news, especially for those who have experienced social oppression. Each part of the body of Christ works with the whole, under the direction of Christ, the head, to reach out with compassion to the world Jesus loves and died for.

Some Christian leaders view teaching about personal piety and social justice as a pendulum that swings back and forth and are concerned that teaching about justice will water down the importance of personal salvation. Scripture teaches that "all our righteous acts are like filthy rags" to God (Isa. 64:6). We cannot earn our way to freedom from sin by working for justice any more than by striving to achieve milestones of personal morality. That's why Jesus died—to set us free, not only from our personal captivity to sin, but from the ways our lives and lifestyles sinfully oppress others. We need a Savior. We recognize that Jesus did the work of salvation for us on the cross, and then we "work out" our salvation, by seeking both personal wholeness and social justice (Phil. 2:12–13).

Carl Ellis points out that our good deeds are not "salvific," meaning they don't accomplish our salvation. They are "doxological," our practical hymns of praise and testimonies of thanksgiving for what God has already done.[9] Or as Jesus put it, "Let your good deeds shine out for all to see, so that everyone will praise your heavenly Father" (Matt. 5:16 NLT).

How to Move Your Church toward Compassion

If you are a pastor or leader of a church that is not yet compassionate to the core, I challenge you to begin your own journey of understanding. Take a vision trip to your local city mission or to a developing country. I rarely talk to a Christian leader who has been on a trip to Africa or India with World Vision or Opportunity International who has not been radically transformed by the experience.

Those of you who are not church leaders can certainly influence the leaders of your congregation by giving them articles and books such as *Compassion, Justice and the Christian Life* by Robert Lupton or *Walking with the Poor* by Bryant Myers and by gathering the funds to send your pastor or leadership team on a vision trip to a developing country. Your pastor is not likely to turn down such a trip and will come back empowered with fresh stories and a broadened understanding of God's work in the world on behalf of the poorest of the poor.

In the Chicago area, Willow Creek Community Church and North Park University have developed trips to the South called Sankofa Trips or Justice Journeys. Participants are asked to find someone of a different race to join them as their partner. They watch videos together as they journey by bus to Memphis, Birmingham, Selma, and other locations, visiting sites where momentous events in the civil rights movement occurred. Trip facilitators engage the group in discussion, and the participants learn from one another along the journey.

In 2005, Bill Hybels, senior pastor of Willow Creek Community Church, asked James Meeks, pastor of Salem Baptist, Chicago's largest black church, to join him on a Justice Journey. Before the trip, Hybels said, "I am one of those prototypical, white educated folks who wondered why there is still a problem. If the laws have been changed and if

Charles

Charles stumbled into Breakthrough for a cup of coffee. We let him eat and shower and "loved him out the door," telling him to come back when he was ready to get help for his addiction.

Then one Sunday, Charles showed up at church. At the end of the service, the pastor asked people to come to the front if they wanted to commit their lives to Christ. I was shocked to see Charles rush to the front and drop to his knees, tears streaming down his face. I joined him as he poured his heart out to the Lord. "God, I can't stop drinking. I need your help. Please come into my life and save me." I also prayed that God would free him and take over his life.

The next day Charles came to Breakthrough sober. It was amazing! We had never seen him sober. But two weeks later we were discouraged when Charles returned drunk again. Over the next months, Charles continued to experience relapses. Frankly, it was the relapses we noticed most, until one of his old drinking buddies commented, "Charles has really changed."

I began to realize he was right. Charles' drinking sprees were becoming shorter and fewer, and his periods of sobriety were getting longer. I hadn't noticed, but his street friends had noticed the change, the new Charles.

Charles is now living sober. He testifies to anyone who cares to listen, "Jesus is my higher power. Without the Lord, I wouldn't be alive today."

everyone's voting and if there is equal opportunity, why is there any lingering difficulty?"[10]

Hybels became intentional about growing in his understanding of social concerns. He wanted to be informed. Recently, his ministry has taken an obvious turn toward a greater emphasis on poverty, AIDS, and global injustice. His conversion to a deeper understanding of social issues is having a huge effect on the hundreds of thousands of people who are influenced by his dynamic leadership.

God is calling the church to action. Young people are more aware than ever of the issues of injustice in the world and are not likely to stay engaged with churches that are becoming increasingly irrelevant to the obvious economic disparities and social injustices across the globe.

There is a story of about a golf ball that landed on the top on an anthill. A novice golfer swung his club and missed the ball, but killed several dozen ants. This happened three or four times. Finally, a worried ant was heard saying to the other remaining ants, "Look, if we're going to survive, we had better get on the ball."

The churches that survive and thrive in the decades to come will be the churches that "get on the ball" when it comes to leading their people into deeper understanding and practice of doing good and righting wrongs in the hurting communities of the world. Instead of asking the spiritual and social change agents in our churches to usher or to serve on multiple committees, we need to be challenging them to discover how God has uniquely wired them to do the good works God has "prepared in advance" for them to do (Eph. 2:10).

Luke 7 reports that John the Baptist sent his disciples to ask Jesus if he was the Son of God or if they should look for another. Jesus' response reflects how people will know that the church understands the whole gospel and is following Jesus by being compassionate to the core. Jesus replied, "Go back and report to John what you have seen and heard: The blind receive sight, the lame walk, those who have leprosy are cured, the deaf hear, the dead are raised, and the good news is preached to the poor" (Luke 7:22).

Our churches will come alive and people will be drawn to become part of the family of God when the church becomes the hands and feet of God reaching out to a hurting world. The world will see our good works and glorify the Father. We need to get on the ball and become compassionate to the core before it is too late.

We All Need a Breakthrough

Like Jesus' inquisitive disciples when confronted with a man born blind, I want answers. "Whose fault is it, Rabbi, that this man was born blind?" Why are children born into poverty? Why is there so much pain and despair in the world? Whose fault is it, Rabbi?

Why are there pockets of hopelessness in the inner city? Why are there young men on the corner with their phones chirping when the police come near? Who sinned, this man, his parents, or society? Why are children in the city stuck in neighborhoods with failing schools and no economic and social skills that will enable them to ever achieve in

> *Breakthrough broke through*
> *my dark night*
> *Breakthrough broke through*
> *to bring the sunlight*
> *I can see my hope on the horizon,*
> *I've been set free*
> *Because Breakthrough broke*
> *through for me.*
>
> —Babbie Mason[1]

the marketplace? Why are there homeless beggars with plastic grocery bags huddled over heat grates, sleeping under bridges, pillaging through dumpsters, walking laboriously over broken sidewalks in search of food and shelter? Why are there lines outside shelters and soup kitchens in the wealthiest country of the world? Whose fault is it, Rabbi?

The closer I have gotten to the soul of the city, the louder the questions have resounded. Who can we blame for the problems of the inner city? Some blame the individual: "Why don't they just get a job, say no to drugs and alcohol, and take responsibility for their own lives?" Others accuse the fathers and mothers for the breakdown of the family, or the government for the lack of funding for social programs that might make a difference.

Conservatives tend to blame the individual and his or her family, citing personal failure and the lack of appropriate family values. Liberals blame systemic racism, social inequalities, and structural evil.

We might blame the church for being silent on social issues and for not being more compassionate. Followers of Christ in the city are often stuck between unbelieving activists and inactive believers. We might even blame God for not caring enough to act on their behalf.

"Every year we have the same discussions over and over, and nobody has any answers," complained a teacher friend as we explored solutions to the dilemma of the failing educational system in the inner city. "How are we supposed to teach kids who are living in a shelter or who have been up all night without supervision? Of course they haven't done their homework! They don't even know where their backpacks are. It makes me want to tear my hair out! You're tempted to feel sorry for them, and let them off the hook, but you know that excusing them will only perpetuate the problem. They need to be told, 'Stop your whining, and do your homework.' If they don't put out the extra effort, they will be hopeless victims trapped forever in the cycle of poverty."

The blaming seems to spiral down into cycles of anger that leave us scratching our heads over the complexity of the issues, overwhelmed by the magnitude of the structures that must be confronted. Is there any system that can move us forward? Is anything working? Are there solutions anywhere?

Jesus' response to the disciples' question about who was at fault for the blind man's troubles is an interesting one. He didn't enter into the blame game at all. He didn't even attempt to answer the blame question. Instead, he claimed there was a bigger story, a breakthrough about to be experienced, a healing about to take place that would never have been experienced apart from this man's great need.

The man's difficulty became an opportunity for God to act. The negative circumstance was turned into a positive experience by the gentle hands of Jesus. A miracle unfolded that brought healing to the nameless blind man. It involved the work of God being displayed in the man's world for all to see. His story would be remembered forever.

"This happened so that the work of God might be displayed in his life," said Jesus. "As long as it is day," he continued, "we must do the work of him who sent me. Night is coming when no one can work. While I am in the world, I am the light of the world" (John 9:3–5).

The great light of the world, the lover of humankind, the model kingdom worker, spit his saliva onto the ground, and with the same dust from which he created humans in the image and likeness of God, he formed a muddy compact, gently placed it against the dark, unseeing eyes of the man born blind, and restored his sight. For the first time in the man's life, the light broke through like the dawn and he exclaimed, "One thing I do know. I was blind but now I see!" (John 9:25).

As I have grown in my understanding of the root causes of poverty and the complex issues surrounding its ugly face, I've become less concerned with knowing whom to blame and more interested in recognizing the breakthroughs, the stories of the miracles that erupt when the light and love of God meet the deepest needs of humankind.

Perhaps doing God's work in the world means we need to spit against the night, to get our hands dirty in the muck and mire of the city as we participate in the Creator's plan to redeem and restore all of creation to the way it's supposed to be, that the work of God will be displayed and the world will take notice. The city, in its profound need, is a great laboratory of the love of God.

Reciprocal Relationships with the Poor

Sue looked at me across the table and made a brave confession. "Before I became a Christian five years ago, I couldn't have cared less about the poor," she said. "I actually felt contempt for them. I felt I had worked hard for everything I had, and they were just lazy. Why don't they just get jobs and make something of themselves? When I met Jesus, my heart began to soften. I am beginning to feel love and compassion. God is changing me in ways I never would have thought possible."

Sue had experienced a shift in her emotions and in her thinking because of her newfound relationship with Jesus. As she began to learn the ways of Jesus and read about God's heart for the poor so evident in Scripture, she began to develop a desire to engage meaningfully with the less fortunate. Sue and her husband enrolled in one of Breakthrough's culture circles where she heard firsthand from people who had lived all of their lives in an impoverished community amid oppression and hatred. She began to lead the charge for her church to become compassionate to the core as she learned from the experiences and perspectives of people who were very different than her. Sue was experiencing a significant breakthrough.

Throughout the twenty years I have been in urban ministry in Chicago, I have heard similar stories over and over. Often, the testimony goes something like this: "I started volunteering with Breakthrough because I wanted to help people who were less fortunate than me. I discovered that I was the one who needed help. I had become arrogant and self-centered. I thought I had so much to give, but I received so much more than I could ever give."

God beckons us to reciprocal relationships with the poor. When we cross bridges to enter into relationships with people living in poverty, the poor gain the benefit of our goodwill and financial support. They are privileged to take advantage of our skill-building programs and supportive relationships that lead to good jobs, housing, schools, and other opportunities, and they experience the relational love that assures them God has not forgotten them in their distress.

In return, urban pilgrims receive the blessing of escaping the controlling powers of self-important and self-promotion. They learn an outward focus in their walk with Jesus. They learn to move beyond fear and prejudice and meet real heroes who are managing to survive joyously in bleak circumstances. The experience changes them.

I have to confess I was surprised to see Gwen at my church. The River City Community Church has a reputation for being very urban. We pledge ourselves to work with the community to develop the neighborhood, and we embrace multi-ethnicity and reconciliation. I knew Gwen's parents. She had grown up in an affluent white suburb with the best education possible and all of the benefits money could buy. I just didn't expect to find her at my church in the inner city.

"I graduated from Northwestern University with an MBA," she said. "But I spent the following summer doing an internship at an inner-city mission in Atlanta, and it wrecked my life. I know I can never go back to my rich, suburban lifestyle."

Curtis

"This is no joke," a Breakthrough staff member snapped. "People are dying out there!" Well, yes, especially on the fringes of society, we too often hear of someone who died, seemingly before their time. But I was shocked to learn that Curtis was one of them.

Curtis was my neighbor. We often talked as we walked our dogs. Every time he saw me, he asked if I had any work for him to do. "Hold on," I always said with a grin as I thought about the future. "Soon the Breakthrough Ministry Center will open, and we're going to have an employment center there to help you get a *real* job."

But Curtis never made it to the grand opening.

Our park had become a testing ground for new mixes of drug chemicals. Neighborhood addicts soon learned they could hang out in the parks and get drugs for free. The pushers were competing to claim that their dope gave the best high. They laced heroin with fentanyl, a pain killer approximately a hundred times more potent than heroin, and handed it out in the park to test it. It was like Russian roulette for the addicts. They might get the best high ever, no high at all, or they might die.

Quietly, without public protest, seventy poor people, street people, drug addicts died of strokes and heart attacks. There was no mention of their plight in the papers or on the nightly news until a prominent suburban family's son bought his fix in the park and became one of the victims.

Curtis was one of the invisible ones.

I've seen it happen over and over. Kids come to the city to work with Breakthrough or another ministry for the summer or a year, and they realize the experience has changed them forever. They can't go back to their former lives. Their priorities have changed. They become borderline obnoxious to the unconverted, pointing out waste and greed, wearing clothing purchased from thrift stores, and talking incessantly about their longing to get back to the front lines of radical mission.

Older adults who have succeeded in the marketplace or climbed the corporate ladder begin to make radical decisions to give away more and more of their income to ministries that care for the poor. They spend their vacation days building houses in developing countries and their weekends serving meals or sorting clothing at homeless shelters. Somewhere along the way, like Gwen and Sue, their comfortable lives have been "wrecked," and they cannot go on with the old status quo. They know they have to live out a new calling, a new worldview.

Ike tells a story about volunteering at Breakthrough's overnight shelter.

One of the guys wanted a wakeup call at five in the morning, so Ike set his watch and woke him up. A few minutes later, Ike was surprised to see the man dressed in a nice suit. He told Ike he was about to take public transportation out to his job in suburban Schaumburg. Why was he living in a shelter if he had a nice white-collar job out in Schaumburg? He had gotten into a disagreement with his wife and had decided to leave home . . . but with no place to go. Ike suddenly realized that he and this homeless man were very much alike. If just a few circumstances had been different, he could have easily been in the same situation as the man in the shelter. It changed Ike's perspective on homelessness and humbled him.

There are various reasons why adventurers like Sue, Gwen, and Ike cannot go back to their old lives of isolation. Many have found among the poor, people whose faith was so forged in the furnaces of adversity that they can still trust God when many of us would melt with fear. Money can provide a semblance of insulation from some problems, but sooner or later we all—even the rich—come to the end of our untried faith and need more experienced warriors to hold us up and show us how to reach out to God. That's when someone who's been through it becomes your best friend. Jesus' first beatitude, "Blessed are the poor in spirit," describes those who know they are nothing without God. But they are so rich in faith that "theirs is the kingdom of heaven" (Matt. 5:3). In most cases, these "poor" people generously share what they do have even with the "rich." Experience friends like that, and you will never want to leave.

When we move out of our social isolation and befriend people in need, we often get in touch with those parts of ourselves that we may have buried and shunned. By avoiding the broken, the addicted, the poor, the mentally ill, the anxious, the hopeless, the helpless, the physically repulsive, the smelly, the deformed, the big, the little, the obnoxious, the frail, the old, the blind, and the lame, we just might be shunning those parts of ourselves that are masked by our education and sophistication. Yet, if we look deeply at ourselves, we can usually find places that relate to the very people we try so creatively to avoid.

King Josiah's Breakthrough

Discovering God's heart for the poor throughout Scripture was, for me, much like the experience of Josiah, a young king whose story is told in the biblical books of 2 Kings, 2 Chronicles, and Jeremiah.

Josiah asked the religious leaders under his reign to clean out the temple. In it, they found scrolls of the Pentateuch, the law of God. They rushed with their newfound treasure to Josiah and read God's Word to him. The high priest, Hilkiah, consulted Huldah, the prophetess, and she warned that calamity would come to the land if the Word of God was not obeyed. When Josiah heard the Word, he tore his robe, put ashes on his head to signify his remorse, and repented.

Later, Jeremiah would write of Josiah, "'He defended the cause of the poor and needy, and so all went well. Is that not what it means to know me?' declares the LORD" (Jer. 22:16). Could it be that we are missing something of what it means to know the Lord by neglecting to listen to and obey the many instructions in Scripture about caring for the poor?

As I read through Scripture while living in an urban context, I began to see how I, like Josiah and the people of his day, had missed the central message of God's good news to the poor. I began to read the overarching message of Scripture and the mission of Jesus on the earth from the perspective of the poor, and it shifted my focus. I had to repent of my neglect and embrace a new way of life.

Like in Josiah's time, many Christians today are discovering huge portions of Scripture that have been neglected, as if lost in the temple for years. As we dust off the Word and read it with new eyes, sensitized by our relationships with hurting people, we are convicted that we have neglected to follow Christ in full obedience in this call to the poor. What do we do with this new information? How do we grow into a new way of living?

Kay Warren, wife of Rick Warren, author of the best-selling *The Purpose Driven Life*, tells the story of a life-changing experience that started when she inadvertently read an article in *Christianity Today* about the twelve million HIV/AIDS orphans in Africa.

> "It was as if I fell off the donkey on the Damascus road because I had no clue. I didn't know one single orphan." For days afterward, she was haunted by that fact: [twelve] million orphans.
>
> Unable to block it from her mind, Kay began to get mad at God, praying, "Leave me alone. Even if it is true, what can I do about it? I'm a white, suburban soccer mom. There is nothing I can do." But that did no good.
>
> After weeks, then months of anguish, she realized she faced a fateful choice. She could either pretend she did not know . . . or she could become personally involved.
>
> "I made a conscious choice to say, 'Yes.' I had a pretty good suspicion that I was saying yes to a bucket load of pain. In that moment, God shattered my heart. He just took my heart and put it through a woodchip machine. My heart came out on the other side in more pieces than I could gather back up in my arms.
>
> "It changed the direction of my life. I will never be the same. Never. I can never go back. I became a seriously disturbed woman."[2]

Kay's husband, Rick, was tentative in his support of his wife's new cause, until he too experienced a breakthrough after visiting Africa and seeing firsthand the devastating impact of poverty and AIDS. He told

Christianity Today he was driven to reexamine Scripture with new eyes. What he found humbled him.

"I found those [two thousand] verses on the poor. How did I miss that? I went to Bible college, two seminaries, and I got a doctorate. How did I miss God's compassion for the poor? I was not seeing all the purposes of God.

"The church is the body of Christ. The hands and feet have been amputated, and we're just a big mouth, known more for what we're against." Warren found himself praying, "God, would you use me to reattach the hands and the feet to the body of Christ, so that the whole church cares about the whole gospel in a whole new way—through the local church?"[3]

Rick came to recognize that the church in America had become spiritually empty. "[People] don't know God made them for a purpose." He began to refocus his message to include care for the poor.[4]

Like Josiah learned, it is not too late. We can change the course of our lives and experience new, transforming breakthroughs through engaging with the poor. It starts with the same humility Josiah displayed and repentance—a turning around, making the choice to take a new direction, to put practices into place that educate us and expose us to the needs of the poor.

Repentance is not a very popular word these days. It assumes we have been thinking or doing something wrong or neglecting something important. Most of us would rather not do the hard work of examining our lives, families, and institutions to see if we may have gotten off course. We like to think we have it all together.

Repentance requires humility, the willingness to take the lower place, the understanding that it is only by God's grace that we are able to rise up each day, clothed and in our right mind.

Humility is a bit elusive because once you think you have arrived at humility, you can be sure you haven't. Instead, it strikes us best when we realize we don't have it all together. When we recognize we need a Savior. We need to be rescued from the mess we are in.

Change is difficult. We don't want to be challenged with the needs of the poor. We feel we have enough on our plates already. But, if we want to grow, we need to change. Are you ready for a transformation? Do you want to grow? Are you willing to change? Josiah was willing to change. He repented in dust and ashes and put into practice what he learned from the Word of God.

It is God's kindness that leads us to repentance. It isn't almighty God wielding a club over our heads to force us to engage with the poor, but the realization that "every good and perfect gift" we have comes from our Father above (James 1:17). When we truly realize how dependant we are upon God for anything good in our lives, we are ready to repent of our self-sufficiency and pride and fall at the feet of our maker in humility and repentance.

Breakthrough Practices

Christians throughout history have adopted practices that have strengthened their relationship with God. In the next seven chapters, I am going to suggest seven breakthrough practices that will make an impact in your life and bring you out of a posture of guilt and confusion regarding the poor and into a place of heartfelt engagement with them. I believe these breakthrough practices will change your life.

First, seek to understand, experience, and pray for the "shalom of God." Jeremiah 29:7 instructs us to "seek the peace [the shalom] and prosperity of the city to which I have carried you into exile. Pray to the

LORD for it, because if it prospers, you too will prosper." When you recognize that our own peace is intricately bound with the peace of the most broken in the world, your prayers and your practices will be transformed.

Second, adopt the practice of presence by making an effort to regularly and intentionally spend time with people who are less fortunate than you. Engaging in relationships will open your heart to compassion and inform your actions.

Third, learn to be guided by the Spirit of God rather than being driven by need. The needs of people in crisis can be overwhelming if we try to fix problems ourselves rather than listening to the still small voice that prompts us to take appropriate actions. "Where the Spirit of the Lord is, there is freedom" (2 Cor. 3:17). Obedience to the nudge of God will free you to care for others out of love and obedience rather than guilt and obligation.

Fourth, understand and practice stewardship. We are stewards, not owners, of the resources God brings our way. Therefore, as Jesus said, "From everyone who has been given much, much will be demanded" (Luke 12:48). How we use our time, talents, and money is an important indicator of what we have our hearts set on. God expects us to invest wisely, to multiply our resources, and to use what we've been given for kingdom purposes.

Fifth, practice discipline. Jesus calls us to take up the cross to follow him. We will not accomplish the good works God has planned for us if we don't adopt lifestyles characterized by goals that are worthwhile and disciplined follow-through. Like Kay Warren learned, we make choices every day that will either lead us deeper into the heart of God for the poor, or will shroud our calloused hearts with more layers of indifference. It requires discipline.

Sixth, join a movement. In an individualistic society, we need to be reminded that we were never expected to be on this journey alone. We were meant to be part of the community of faith, the ever expanding body of Christ on the earth, in which we each have a significant role to play, yet we are connected to the whole. We can do so much more when we work together in unity.

Seventh, grow in racial understanding. The foundation of generational poverty is often rooted in racial oppression and inequality. We need to understand our privilege and how it has affected others less fortunate. Our hearts are broken by the racial injustice experienced by our brothers and sisters. We repent and take up the cause of racial justice.

Like Sue, Gwen, Ike, Kay, and Rick, the breakthrough practices outlined in this book will change you forever. As we grow together in this amazing journey toward understanding God's heart for the poor, we will learn that God also loves us in our poverty of soul. Together we become beggars who have found bread, and we begin to break bread together in the fellowship of the Spirit of God. We all need a breakthrough of the love of God in our hearts.

The Breakthrough of Shalom

One of my favorite movies is *Crash*. Its tangled plot weaves together the stories of strangers in Los Angeles, following them over a thirty-six-hour period through a series of events including a collision, a carjacking, and a shooting, among other things. The movie highlights the racial attitudes and tensions that sometimes rise to the surface as we crash into one another in the course of our lives.

We are all a mixture of positive and negative character attributes. We all have prejudices as a result of our upbringing and life experiences. When our lives intersect with people who are different from us, our deep-seated beliefs are often exposed. When people from different backgrounds and perspectives interact with one another in community, they tend to crash.

Jesus addressed how we are to live together in

> *True peace is not merely the absence of tension; it is the presence of justice.*
>
> —Dr. Martin Luther King, Jr.[1]

this world of clashing cultures, priorities, and perspectives in the Beatitudes at the beginning of the Sermon on the Mount (Matt. 5:1–12). He describes what a community under the reign of God should look like.

In verse 9, Jesus says, "Blessed are the peacemakers, for they will be called children of God" (TNIV). It is when we put our faith in Christ and his redemptive work on the cross that we become children of God, but one of the clear indications that we have become children of God is how we work to make peace in relationships that would ordinarily crash.

Peace is also a theme in Isaiah's prophecy of the birth of Jesus: "For to us a child is born, to us a son is given, and the government will be on his shoulders. And he will be called Wonderful Counselor, Mighty God, Everlasting Father, Prince of Peace. Of the increase of his government and peace there will be no end" (Isa. 9:6–7). Jesus would come and lead the world to peace. He would break down the walls that divide us and bring us together in a life of harmony and right relationships. Jesus is the Prince of Peace and instructs us to be peacemakers.

The Hebrew word for peace in the Old Testament is *shalom*. In Jewish culture, still today, people greet one another with the word *shalom*. Our English word *peace* doesn't do justice to the richness conveyed by the Hebrew term, which means much more: completeness, safety, welfare, soundness, contentment, tranquility, and harmony.

Cornelius Plantinga writes:

The webbing together of God, humans, and all creation in justice, fulfillment, and delight is what the Hebrew prophets call *shalom*. We translate it peace, but it means far more than mere peace of mind or a cease-fire between enemies. In the Bible, shalom means *universal flourishing, wholeness, and delight*—a rich state of affairs in which natural needs are satisfied and natural gifts fruitfully employed, a state of affairs that inspires joyful wonder as its Creator and Savior opens doors and welcomes the creatures in whom he delights. Shalom, in other words, is the way things ought to be.[2]

Timothy Keller describes shalom as "the way things ought to be." When God created the world, he laid it out like a garment made out of cloth (Ps. 102:25–26). A piece of fabric for a garment is made up of thousands of threads woven together. The higher the thread count, the richer and stronger the fabric. The world God created is billions of entities intricately woven together by God, with interdependence and harmony. The work of social justice is to participate in God's work to reweave the fabric of creation.[3]

Keller suggests the best way to understand shalom is to look at what happens when it is absent. When everything in your body, for instance, is working together in harmony, you are healthy and experience physical shalom. But when a disease prevents the parts of your body from working together as they should, your body breaks down and you lose that shalom.

We can also think about psychological shalom. When my mind, conscience, passions, and actions are all in harmony, I experience psychological shalom. However, when I do something my conscience says I shouldn't, there is a disconnect, and my conscience begins to scold. I begin to unravel, and I lose my internal shalom.[4]

Socially, when those with money, power, influence, status, and connections begin to weave their resources into the social fabric of the community by investing in housing, education, and the welfare of all people, the frayed ends and torn remnants of fabric are rewoven into the whole. People in the community are supported by its stronger, rewoven, social fabric. Some people may end up with more and some less, but we all have what we need: good schools, safe parks, places to live.

Keller uses the example of the little town of Bedford Falls in the classic movie *It's a Wonderful Life*. The main character, George Bailey, runs a savings and loan that weaves resources into the community by giving loans, even when people might not be able to pay them back. The company has been patient and hasn't foreclosed even when people were not able to pay back their loans.

Over the years, the Bailey family sacrificed for the sake of the community, and their "weaving" of investment held the town together. As time passes, George Bailey gets depressed, and he tells Clarence the angel he wishes he was never born. So Clarence shows George what the town would be like if he had not been in the picture. Mr. Potter, greedy and selfish in his dealings, runs the town, which is now called Potterville instead of Bedford Falls. The town is marred by poverty, prostitution, and degradation. Its social fabric is unraveling.

Reweaving the Fabric of Shalom

To do justice is to reweave the fabric of shalom, to go to those places where the fabric of society has unraveled and do what we can to repair it. We invest our time, energy, and money into society because it builds the shalom of God.

Proverbs 3:27–28 says, "Do not withhold good from those who deserve it, when it is in your power to act. Do not say to your neighbor, 'Come back later; I'll give it tomorrow'—when you now have it with you." When people get greedy and quit reaching out to those in need, when they quit caring about each other, we lose social shalom.

The loss of neighborhood shalom eventually leads to crime, poverty, racial tension, and gang wars. This is not what God intended for the world. Those of us who are the children of God will participate in God's work in the world to restore shalom.

Concerning the Beatitudes, Richard Rohr wrote:

Jesus is teaching that *right relationship* is the ultimate and daily criterion. If a social order allows and encourages, and even mandates, good connectedness between people and creation, people and events, people and people, people and God, then you would have a truly sacred culture: the Reign of God. The world as it would be if God were directly in charge would be a world of right relationship. It would not be a world with pain or mystery but simply a world where we would be in good contact with all things, where we would be connected and in communion. Conversely, the work of the Evil One is always to separate, divide and throw apart.[5]

Jesus taught that all of the commandments could be summed into two. We are to love the Lord our God with all our heart, mind, and strength, and to love our neighbor as ourselves (Mark 12:28–31). This vertical and horizontal focus can be symbolized by the vertical and horizontal bars of the cross of Christ. At the center is a heart of love. Jesus died to reconcile us to God and to one another. He has given us a ministry of reconciliation, bringing others to God and into right relationships with their brothers and sisters so they can lead lives characterized by God's love.

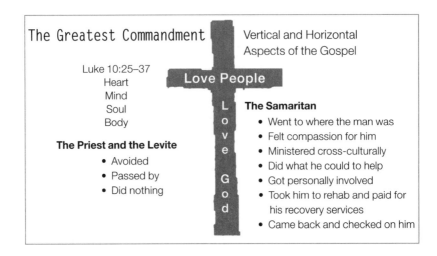

The Greatest Commandment — Vertical and Horizontal Aspects of the Gospel

Luke 10:25–37
Heart
Mind
Soul
Body

Love People

The Priest and the Levite
- Avoided
- Passed by
- Did nothing

Love God

The Samaritan
- Went to where the man was
- Felt compassion for him
- Ministered cross-culturally
- Did what he could to help
- Got personally involved
- Took him to rehab and paid for his recovery services
- Came back and checked on him

Western Christians have tended to interpret the term *righteousness* in a very individualistic, personal way. We think of righteousness in terms of how we are doing personally in keeping the commandments and staying in right relationship with God. The Greek word for righteousness, *dikaiosune*, carries within it the meaning of the word *justice*. Therefore, to "seek first the kingdom of God and His righteousness" (Matt. 6:33 NKJV) means to seek both personal morality and social justice.

Would it change your understanding of the Scripture verses below if you replaced the Greek word *dikaiosune* with the word *justice*?

- "But seek first his kingdom and his [*justice*], and all these things will be given to you as well" (Matt. 6:33).
- "Peacemakers who sow in peace raise a harvest of [*justice*]" (James 3:18).
- "Blessed are those who are persecuted because of [*justice*], for theirs is the kingdom of heaven" (Matt. 5:10).

The Righteousness Window

Theologian and author Carl Ellis describes the meaning of the word *righteousness* by using a quadrant diagram he calls the "Righteousness Window."[6] He teaches that righteousness is relational and covenantal and includes both our vertical relationship with God and our horizontal relationships with others.

The Righteousness Window

	Godliness	Justice
Personal	**Personal Godliness** 1 Peter 3:15 2 Corinthians 5:17	**Personal Justice** Micah 6:8 Jeremiah 22:16 Proverbs 31:8–9
Social	**Social Godliness** 2 Chronicles 7:14 Joshua 24:15 Acts 16:29–34	**Social Justice** Amos 4:1–2; 5:10–15, 24 Isaiah 10:1–4

In the top left-hand quadrant is *personal godliness*. My personal relationship with God is vitally important. I spend time in daily prayer, meditation, and Scripture study in order to draw near to God, to listen, and to lay out my life before the him. I have a personal relationship with God that needs to be nurtured, and so I engage in daily practices toward that end.

In the top right-hand quadrant is *personal justice*. This has to do with my relationships with others. Having right relationships with others is evidence of God's righteousness being worked into me and lived out through me. The apostle John teaches this clearly, identifying our relationship with others as a test of true conversion: "We know that we have passed from death to life, because we love each other" (1 John 3:14 TNIV).

In the next chapter, he explains: "If we say we love God yet hate a brother or sister, we are liars. For if we do not love a fellow believer, whom we have seen, we cannot love God, whom we have not seen. And he has given us this command: Those who love God must also love one another" (1 John 4:20–21 TNIV).

The prophet Isaiah wrote about people who were seeking to get near God but their prayers fell on deaf ears.

> "Why have we fasted," they say, "and you have not seen it? Why have we humbled ourselves, and you have not noticed?" Yet on the day of your fasting, you do as you please and exploit all your workers. Your fasting ends in quarreling and strife, and in striking each other with wicked fists. You cannot fast as you do today and expect your voice to be heard on high. (Isa. 58:3–4)

I didn't think I was exploiting my workers until I began to learn how unfair trade and production practices hurt many of the people who produce the goods and services I purchase every day. Could it be that my choice of the coffee I drink, the clothing I wear, or the chocolate I consume might be oppressing workers in other parts of the world? Could this affect God's ability to hear and answer my prayers? For each of us, righteousness involves not only our vertical relationship with God (personal godliness) but our horizontal relationships with others (personal justice).

We also participate in groups—families, institutions, churches, organizations, and other affiliations. Ellis calls our righteous behavior expressed through these groups *social godliness* (the lower left-hand quadrant). As participants in these institutions we should expect our leaders to lead us as a group to follow God. Joshua told the Israelites, "Choose for yourselves this day whom you will serve . . . . But as for *me and my household*, we will serve the LORD" (Josh. 24:15, emphasis added).

Those of us who are leaders need to take seriously the responsibility we have been given to lead the people under our influence to live righteously, not only in their personal lives, but as a group. As the leader of the growing family of Breakthrough Urban Ministries, I need to follow the lead of Joshua in declaring, "As for me and Breakthrough, we will serve the Lord."

This understanding of group decisions and corporate acts is more common in the East than in the West. I asked a friend who grew up in India and converted from Hinduism to Christianity how his family had reacted to his decision to follow Jesus. He looked at me perplexed for a minute and then responded, "Oh, we all came to faith in Christ together!" Much like the experience of the Philippian jailor and his family in Acts 16, my friend's entire family made the decision together to follow God. This corporate way of coming to faith in Christ is very foreign to most of us in the U.S., where our thinking is more individualistic.

Fred

"I guess I'm one of the lucky ones," Fred remarked as we folded warm towels in the back room of the center.

There was nothing about Fred's life that would lead me to describe him as lucky. He had told me about being beaten regularly by his alcoholic father. Multiple experiences of physical and sexual abuse had scarred him deeply. He had spent his entire adult life in and out of rehab centers, jails, and hospitals for his alcoholism.

"What makes you say you're lucky?" I asked.

"Did you watch the news about John Wayne Gacy's execution this morning?"

Of course I had. It was the top news story of the day. People had cheered when they heard Gacy was dead. He had lured young men, many of them homeless like Fred, into his house. He raped and murdered thirty-three of them, burying them in a crawl space under his house or tossing their bodies in the Des Plaines River.

"I was there, with him in his house," Fred said quietly. "I'm really lucky, cuz I got out."

The last I heard, Fred is sober again after being severely injured in a fall down a flight of stairs and nearly freezing to death in the park. Even when he's not sober, Fred gives credit to God for getting him through each day. He truly believes he is one of the lucky ones.

The fourth quadrant in the righteousness window is *social justice*—how we as a people group relate to other people groups. How do we treat people who are different from us? Those who are outside our families, churches, institutions, race, or class? How are "my people" treating others? What can I do either to rise up as a leader or to influence the leaders of groups in which I participate to treat others with the love of God?

As a descendent of German immigrants, I wept for hours after watching the movie *Schindler's List*. Though I didn't live in Germany during the Holocaust, I was touched deeply by the profound injustice my ancestors had committed against the Jews. Dietrich Bonhoeffer, a pastor and theologian who lived in Germany during that period, recognized that his faith required him to take a stand for justice and lead his people to resist the Nazi regime. He was eventually imprisoned and executed.

William Wilberforce, as noted previously, led the charge in Britain to abolish the slave trade. A committed Christian, Wilberforce recognized that his faith required him to use his leadership ability to bring about social change, not merely how he personally related to other people.

Second Peter 2:7–9 says Lot was a righteous man who was "distressed by the filthy lives of lawless men (for that righteous man, living among them day after day, was tormented in his righteous soul by the lawless deeds he saw and heard)." I like the Revised Standard Version, which says "he was vexed in his righteous soul day after day with their lawless deeds."

When God decided to destroy Sodom and Gomorrah because of their wickedness, Lot's uncle, Abraham, was able to barter with God and garner a commitment that if ten righteous people could be found in the cities, God would spare Sodom and Gomorrah. Even though Lot was called a righteous man, he had not been able to influence others to join him to take a stand against the injustices of the cities.

Because Lot had not been able to mobilize even ten people in Sodom and Gomorrah to live godly lives, their entire cities were destroyed. The people of Sodom and Gomorrah have been remembered not only because of their sexual deviance, but also because they "were arrogant, overfed and unconcerned; they did not help the poor and needy" (Ezek. 16:49). Today we don't have leadership books written about Lot.

On the other hand, dozens of books have been written about the life and leadership of Nehemiah. Nehemiah saw the distress of the city of Jerusalem and started a movement to bring about change. He garnered resources from the government, conducted a reconnaissance mission to survey the problem, and mobilized a movement of people to rebuild the walls of Jerusalem. When he heard the outcry of the poor, he became angry, "called together a large meeting," and told their oppressors, "What you are doing is not right. Shouldn't you walk in the fear of our God?" (Neh. 5:6–9). Nehemiah and his people have become known as "Repairer[s] of Broken Walls, Restorer[s] of Streets with Dwellings," just as Isaiah promised (Isa. 58:12). He organized a movement.

Social justice is not something we can do by ourselves. It involves starting or joining a movement of people who are acting together to bring about change in systems and structures. It requires that we work together. When we hear and feel the passion of Christ for the poor, we begin to act together to confront the principalities and the powers that are oppressing people. We get to do it together, each using our unique gifts.

Just being vexed in our righteous souls over wickedness will not save our cities. Like Nehemiah, we need to organize a kingdom movement and help people find their places at the walls, hammer in one hand and sword in the other, prepared for battle, but staying on task until the job is done. Dietrich Bonhoeffer, William Wilberforce, John Wesley, and Dorothy Day were kingdom movement leaders. They integrated their personal faith with their social outreach and care for the poor and oppressed.

The Unrighteousness Window

Ellis describes the reverse of the Righteousness Window and calls it the "Unrighteousness Window."[7] This is the picture of a world without the shalom of God, where covenant relationships between individuals and God and between one another are violated and broken. A world characterized by individual and institutional ungodliness and oppression is not the way it's supposed to be. Only the cross of Christ can free us from this bondage to sin and set us on the path of righteousness.

As I mentioned earlier, Jesus summed up the most important commandments by focusing on love that is vertical and horizontal: "Love the Lord your God with all your heart and with all your soul and with all your mind . . . Love your neighbor as yourself" (Matt. 22:37, 39). Interestingly, the two sins that are most emphasized in Scripture are idolatry and lack of care for the poor. We worship idols when we place anything above God in our lives, violating our vertical relationship with God. Lack of care for the poor is evidence that we are violating our horizontal relationships and failing to love our neighbor as ourselves.

The Unrighteousness Window

	Ungodliness	Oppression
Individual	**Individual Ungodliness** When a person sins and suffers the consequences	**Individual Oppression** When a person sins and forces others to suffer the consequences
Institutional	**Institutional Ungodliness** When a society sins and suffers the consequences	**Institutional Oppression** When a society sins and forces others to suffer the consequences

When a person sins and suffers the consequences, he or she experiences *individual ungodliness*. This is the aspect of sin that the church has focused on in recent history. It has to do with our personal choices that violate our covenant relationship with God and lead to rebellion, self-centeredness, and immorality. When we look to something or someone to take the place of God in our lives, we will always be disappointed, and we will personally suffer the consequences. When we put anything or anyone in the place of God, we are practicing idolatry.

When a person sins and forces others to suffer the consequences, the result is *individual oppression*. Many of the guests who come to Breakthrough have been victims of oppression in multiple ways through childhood neglect and abusive relationships. When our actions cause harm to others, we are practicing individual injustice and oppression.

Jean, who still struggles with addiction and continually falls into relationships with abusive men, told me she was born a drug baby to a heroin-addicted mother:

When I was nine years old, my mom would put lipstick and perfume on me and let men feel me up. If I resisted, she'd throw me in a closet and lock the door. When I was eleven, my stepfather raped me. I had to have twenty-one stitches—ten inside, eleven outside. At the age of twelve, I went to foster care. My foster parents were real good to me, but they passed away when I was eighteen, so then I was on my own.

I went back with my mom, the one who had abused me. My stepfather wanted to have sex with me. I told my mother, but she didn't believe me, as always.

I got married when I was twenty-one, but my husband was physically abusive. He used to tie me down on the bed and hit me with a belt. At twenty-three, I started smoking marijuana, but I wanted something stronger to dull the pain in my life, so I started sniffing airplane glue and spray paint. I left my husband at age twenty-six and started up with this man named Tony. But he abused me, too. He used to beat me and put me on the corner to sell my body. By this time, I also started tooting [snorting] heroin.

Certainly Jean has made choices that have led to individual ungodliness, and she is on the path of repentance from her personal ungodliness. But she is also the victim of severe individual oppression that has scarred her for life. She needs to experience the loving support of caring relationships in order to heal the pain that was brought upon her by others.

When a society sins and suffers the consequences, we have *institutional ungodliness*. The letters to the churches in the book of Revelation are good examples of God confronting institutional ungodliness. Local churches were told they had left their first love—not just errant individuals within the church who needed correction, but the church as a whole. They had become lukewarm and were tolerating false teaching and immorality. Once they had a reputation of being alive, but now they were dead. Others were commended for their faithfulness in the face of suffering, for their love and faith, service and perseverance.

But when a society sins and forces others to suffer the consequences, the result is *institutional oppression*. This has to do with structures and systems that oppress the poor and perpetuate injustice. The prophet Amos warned the "women who oppress the poor and crush the needy" (Amos 4:1). He lamented, "You trample on the poor," and "deprive the poor of justice in the courts" (Amos 5:11–12).

Social injustice is very evident in the community in which I live on the west side of Chicago. Generational poverty that breeds a culture of hopelessness is rooted back to the history of slavery, unjust legislation, and unfair lending and housing practices that excluded entire groups of people from opportunity for advancement. Many of the schools in our community are failing to prepare their students for jobs in the marketplace, in part because they lack the financial resources and the social will to thrive. Our community has been labeled a "food desert" because of the lack of access to fresh meat and produce. Hospitals have been closed under the weight of the uninsured who used emergency rooms as their only access to healthcare.

These issues are large and complex. They demand creative thought and new ideas. The shalom of God can and will come to a community like ours when the church of Christ understands the call to seek the shalom of the city, to pray for it, work for it, and live it together in community. The broken strands in the social fabric of the community can be mended as Christians join together to reach out in love to right the wrongs of social oppression.

The kingdom of God is a kingdom characterized by shalom. Jesus told us to pray, "your kingdom come, your will be done on earth as it is in heaven" (Matt. 6:10–19). The kingdom of God will come in its fullness when Jesus returns, but in the meantime, God has commissioned us to love God and love people, and to seek the shalom of the city, to "let justice roll on like a river, righteousness like a never-failing stream!" (Amos 5:24).

The last part of Isaiah 65 gives a portrait of life when God's kingdom is finally established on the earth. The city will be a delight. There will be no more crying or infant mortality. People will live long, productive lives in their own homes. They will have an abundance of good food and will enjoy fruitful labor. They will have intimate communication with God and will be blessed. Even the animals will live in peace with one another. This is the way it is supposed to be.

The Breakthrough of Presence

Just Sit There

Tom was nervous the first time he arrived in the church basement to volunteer at Breakthrough's men's shelter. He sat quietly in a room filled with sleeping men for several hours. When the next volunteer arrived to take his place in the early morning, he walked home. Tom told me that he talked to God as he was walking. "Lord, what was that about? All I did was sit there."

Hearing the voice of the Holy Spirit was new to Tom back then, but he says he heard God respond to him clearly in his thoughts with the

> *Go to the people. Live among them. Learn from them. Love them. Start with what they know. Build on what they have. But of the best leaders, when their task is done, the people will remark, "We have done it ourselves."*
>
> —Chinese poem

words, "What you did was a very good thing, and I appreciate it very much." Tom was hooked and has become one of Breakthrough's regular volunteers. It all started when he showed up to "just sit there."

Drop the Ice

Kent and Pam Lack have been longtime friends of Breakthrough. Kent recalls his first volunteer experience:

It all started when they sent me out for ice that cold, winter night. Coming from the suburbs, I was not familiar with the dark alleys that were there by the church. As timing would have it, all the doors to the church were still locked, and I was carrying four large bags of ice. The last doors that I checked were in the back by the alley. As I turned around, two large men approached, and fear took over me. After hurriedly making my way between the two men, the Holy Spirit prompted me to drop the ice bags and give both men a hug. Once I did, all the inner fear completely left me, and the barriers were removed between the men and me. It was not until later that I would learn the men were coming to the meal that night at Breakthrough.

Both Tom and Kent took brave steps simply to show up at a homeless shelter in the city. They didn't know what to expect, but they were willing to be present in the lives of hurting people. For both of them, the simple first step was the breakthrough of *presence*. Kent's story reminds us that when we put ourselves in situations that are outside our comfort zone, God begins to melt our cold hearts. Symbolically, we are asked to "drop the ice" and embrace hurting people.

Participant Observation

Anthropologists have developed a technique for learning about cultures called *participant observation*. According to Wikipedia, participant observation is "a research strategy . . . [that aims] to gain a close and intimate familiarity with a given group of individuals (such as a religious, occupational, or sub cultural group, or a particular community) and their practices through an intensive involvement with people in their natural environment, often though not always over an extended period of time."[1]

Using participant observation as a research method, anthropologists attempt to participate as fully as they can in a particular culture. They take copious notes during their research and create ethnographies that describe the culture from an insider's perspective.

Participant observation is a great way to begin the journey toward engaging with the poor in meaningful ways. Instead of thinking we know what people want or need and jumping in to help, we sit with them and learn from them. We listen with respect as they share about their journeys and perspectives. Like the old proverb advises, we refuse to judge until we have walked a mile in their shoes.

I remember the early days of Breakthrough when I started serving coffee in the church storefront room. I was amazed by the stories I heard as I asked questions and listened to the men and women who came through the doors. I began to realize that, while many of them were experiencing the consequences of bad decisions they had made, there usually was also a story in the background of their lives that involved the sins of others that had been perpetrated against them.

Women who are out on the street selling their bodies for cash almost always have a history of sexual abuse as very young children. I have never heard a five-year-old say she wants to be a prostitute when she grows up. Many with criminal records for violent acts tell harrowing stories of living in violent environments during their childhoods. When we listen to these kinds of stories over and over again, we grow in our understanding of the root causes of much of the brokenness that people experience, and it softens our hearts toward them.

I remember getting to know Betty and the effects of childhood abuse she experienced. Betty was a regular guest in the early days of our drop-in center. Although she was fifty-two years old, she had the emotional maturity of about an eight-year-old. She ran us ragged with her child-like demands.

To keep her busy, I asked her to cut up greeting-card pictures and paste Bible verses on them so we could send them to a clinic in Africa to be used by missionaries as gifts for the children. She carefully stored her cards in a box when we closed the center at night and went directly to the box the next morning. Betty was proud of her work and showed up every day for the food, friendship, and her job.

But one day something unexpected happened. Someone had moved Betty's box. She began screaming in a fit of rage.

"Where is my box? Who moved my box?"

Finally someone found the box and retrieved it for her. She clutched the box and screamed, "This is mine. Don't touch what's mine!"

We rolled our eyes and shook our heads. That was Betty. She was a little crazy!

Later that day, I was driving Betty to an appointment, and she turned to me and with her little childlike voice said, "Arloa, when I was eight my daddy used me." I began to understand why Betty was stuck at age eight. And why she would cling to her box and scream, "This is mine. Don't touch what's mine."

Being with people in a personal, relational way is the first step toward understanding them and really knowing how we can best serve them. It is the practice of presence.

Following the Example of Jesus

This practice of presence is consistent with the example of Jesus.

> Who, being in very nature God, did not consider equality with God something to be grasped, but made himself nothing, taking the very nature of a servant, being made in human likeness. And being found in appearance as a man, he humbled himself and became obedient to death—even death on a cross! (Phil. 2:6–8)

Jesus had it all: riches, power, and control. Everything was his and at his command. His power was so great that it exploded into stars and planets. His very presence was overwhelming. Everything around him was moved to hushed silence or rocked by tempestuous storms. He created it all with just a word. He commanded everything. He ruled. He was intimate with God. He was equal with God. He was God.

Jesus willingly left all of that power and position behind to become the most vulnerable human being imaginable, a naked baby born into poverty, to an unwed, teen mother in a working class family (Luke 2:4–7). As a newborn, he could not walk or talk or even roll over by himself. He was entirely dependent upon the care of others to feed him and clothe him, to protect him from the evil and violence of the world—from the dark forces of nature that could freeze, trample, or maul him. He needed to be held, warmed, and loved. Can you imagine a more vulnerable or fragile being than a newborn baby?

He grew up like any other kid. His bones developed and he learned to walk and talk. He, who is infinite wisdom, became a learner. He humbled himself and listened and learned to obey authority. He experienced being hungry and tired and tempted.

Sam

"Can you please help our son?" It was a desperate plea from distraught parents. I felt for them, knowing that if my child were homeless in Chicago, I would do anything I could think of to bring him to safety. They must have felt so helpless, knowing their son was living in a wooded forest preserve on the edge of the city. He and his drinking buddies lived on animals they managed to capture in the woods and cook over an open fire.

The Reynolds, who lived in Cleveland, had heard me on the radio when I spoke at Moody Bible Institute's Founder's Week. They called to ask if I could find their son, Sam. The only person they knew who had contact with Sam was the owner of a liquor store. They called him, and before long, Sam was at our door, still drunk, but ready for a change. After several months at Breakthrough, God gave Sam freedom from alcohol. Sam was able to get a job at a local lumber yard and even shared his testimony at Founder's Week the following year.

Sam continues to struggle with drinking. But as Proverbs 24:16 says, "Though a righteous man falls seven times, he rises again." Sam has moved to Florida to live in a mission house where he can continue to get help and rise again.

God "so loved" the world that he sent Jesus to the earth to live among us, to experience our pain, and to teach us how to live as an insider.

Jesus came to the earth to be near the poor, the prisoners, the blind, and the oppressed, to bring them redemption by participating in their pain. He gathered a band of unlikely comrades around himself and poured his life into them. He shared his deepest love, wisdom, cares, and concerns with them, knowing they would betray him, deny him, and abandon him in his time of greatest need.

He reached out to people in pain by spending most of his time with people out on the streets. By his touch or his word they were restored to wholeness. He hung out with the outcasts of his day, the swindlers and drunkards, the overeaters and the sexually immoral. He invited himself over to the home of a despised tax collector so they could eat together in a gesture of cultural friendship. He so closely associated with alcoholics and overeaters that he was accused of being a drunkard and a glutton (Matt. 11:19). He let a woman with a sordid reputation wash his feet with her hair (Luke 7:36–39)! He was not afraid to get close to the outcasts of society.

Even his family and the religious people of Jesus' day accused him of being a lunatic and heretic (Mark 3:20–22). They tried to run him out of town. Powerful people said he was demon-possessed and plotted to kill him (Luke 4:28–29).

Jesus even identified with people who were homeless, claiming that though foxes have holes and birds have nests, he did not have a place to lay his head at night (Matt. 8:20). He understood the vulnerability of having no place to call your own.

Indeed, if Jesus' story of the sheep and the goats were a stand-alone story, Christians would be primarily busy feeding, clothing, visiting prisoners, and taking in strangers. It would almost seem that eternal destiny rests upon what is done for "the least of these" (Matt. 25:31–46). Our foremost concern would be to engage in the lives of the less fortunate, to listen to their stories, and to know their families. Instead, Christians often build barriers of isolation and exclusion and have very little interaction with those from another racial group or social class.

As we go through painful struggles ourselves and as we come alongside others in their pain, we can know for certain that there is nothing we experience that Jesus does not understand as an insider, as one of us.

The trials Jesus experienced surpassed anything we will ever face. He practiced "presence" with us so he can legitimately come alongside us in anything we may have to endure. We follow the model of Jesus when we become present to people who are hurting. As much as we can, we enter into the world of the people we are trying to reach and come alongside them with a message of hope.

Jesus humbled himself and lived the life of a servant. He was obedient to death on a cross where he was brutally flogged and stripped of his clothes. With blood trickling down from the thorns boring into his skull, he felt the weight of the sin and darkness of the entire world. He clearly wanted us to follow his example in love when he proclaimed, "Greater love has no one than this, that he lay down his life for his friends" (John 15:13).

"Jesus relocated," says Wayne Gordon of the Christian Community Development Association. "He became one of us. He didn't commute back and forth to heaven. Jesus knew his people's experiences because he walked and talked with them, knew their struggles, and personally connected with those who were down and out."[2]

Crossing the Road

Jesus' story of the Good Samaritan demonstrates, among other things, his concern with religion that neglects the poor. In the story, an inquisitive lawyer asked Jesus what he must do to inherit eternal life. Jesus used the Socratic method of teaching, returning his question with more questions: "What is written in the Law? . . . How do you read it?"

The attorney answered, "'Love the Lord your God with all your heart and with all your soul and with all your strength and with all your mind . . . Love your neighbor as yourself" (Luke 10:26–27).

Jesus affirmed his answer, then told a story to further illustrate—the story of a man who ministered cross-culturally to the victim of a violent crime. While two religious leaders passed the victim by, the Samaritan "came where the man was; and when he saw him, he took pity on him" (Luke 10:33). In order to experience the compassion of God for hurting people, Christians must go to be near them. We will not experience feelings of compassion for the marginalized of society if we remain isolated from them.

The Greek word translated *pity* in this story is the same one translated *compassion* in Matthew 9:36: "When he [Jesus] saw the crowds, he had compassion on them, because they were harassed and helpless, like sheep without a shepherd." The word is *splagcnivzomai*. The *splagchnon*—the abdomen, womb, or bowels—was considered to be the seat of one's strongest emotions. To have *splagcnivzomai* was to be moved in the *splagchnon*. Both Jesus and the Samaritan man in Jesus' story were moved by compassion when they saw people in need.

When I heard the meaning of this Greek word for compassion, I was immediately reminded of what it was like for me after the birth of my babies. When a newborn baby cries, there is an immediate physiological reaction within a caring mother. Her abdomen instinctively and often painfully contracts, and she feels a strong compulsion to reach out and draw the crying baby into her arms and to her breasts. It is automatic and powerful. Those of you who have given birth have experienced this.

The same, I believe, is true for all who have within them the compassionate heart of God. We cannot resist the cry of human need. It reaches into the deepest parts of us and requires that we respond. It is automatic, and the call to action is powerful. That is why the practice of presence, just going to where hurting people are, will change your life if you know Jesus. You will be compelled to action.

"He went to him and bandaged his wounds" (Luke 10:34). The Samaritan man tenderly and compassionately met the broken man's physical needs and then took him to a rehabilitation center and paid for his entire rehabilitation. His presence to the broken man's needs led to compassionate action on the man's behalf.

When Jesus finished telling this story contrasting the Samaritan man who was a neighbor with the religious leaders who walked past without helping, Jesus gave the religious leaders a severe scolding, using some of the strongest language he could muster. He called them "whitewashed tombs" and pronounced seven "woes" upon them.

Now then, you Pharisees clean the outside of the cup and dish, but inside you are full of greed and wickedness. You foolish people! Did not the one who made the outside make the inside also? But give what is inside the dish to the poor, and everything will be clean for you. Woe to you Pharisees, because you give God a tenth of your mint, rue and all other kinds of garden herbs, but you neglect justice and the love of God. You should have practiced the latter without leaving the former undone. (Luke 11:39–42)

Jesus clearly valued acts of justice and dismissed empty piety. The difference is that the Samaritan man, who became the good neighbor, was willing to cross over to the other side of the road and become present to the mugged man.

My Experience with Being Invisible

I experienced the breakthrough of presence when I was taking an anthropology class at the Lincoln Christian University's urban extension program in Chicago. For one of the projects we were required to conduct our own participant observation and write an *ethnography* (a paper describing a particular culture). Since I was already working with homeless men and women at Breakthrough, I chose to try to experience what it was like to be homeless, so I volunteered to mimic a homeless woman for four days.

I walked through pouring rain and finally found sanctuary in a Catholic church. After sitting through mass, I asked the priest if he knew where I could find shelter for the night. He gave me an address and sent me walking five miles to the south side of Chicago to find shelter. The address he gave me proved to be incorrect, but after asking questions of passersby, I finally arrived at the shelter door. I was abruptly turned away with the words, "This is not that kind of shelter." I began walking around again, not sure what to do next.

Finally, at about eleven at night, after having been followed by a pimp and offered drugs, a policeman directed me to a shelter that took me in. I woke the next day on a mat on the floor of a storefront church with thirty other women. Women were crying, arguing, and talking to themselves. Many of them were sick with colds and coughed throughout the night. There was one toilet and shower for all of us. There was no toilet paper, towels, or soap.

For breakfast, we were given a little glob of cooked oatmeal with no milk or sugar. We ate out of little plastic margarine containers. There was no coffee or juice. The women exchanged bummed cigarettes for amoxicillin and aspirin. I recognized that these women were the lucky ones. Others had to spend the night in abandoned buildings or under bridges or had found someone who would take them in for the night, often at a big price.

The women in the shelter told me where I could get meals: coffee and a donut at one ministry, lunch there at noon, dinner at a Catholic church, and then I could join them back at the shelter for a skimpy chicken leg and a little rice or cooked beans. None of the staff in the places we went for food and shelter ever asked my name or what I needed to get back on my feet.

I remember standing in line for dinner at the Catholic church and watching as well-dressed teachers and social workers from the adjoining school walked past us without looking at us. It was as if we were looking through a one-way window. We could see them, but they couldn't see us. Experiencing the feelings of being invisible and of worrying where I would sleep and what I would eat helped me to understand the plight of the homeless from an entirely different perspective. It changed me forever.

When I went back to my role at Breakthrough, I did so with a deeper understanding of how important it was to look people in the eyes, to know their names, to hear their stories, and to respect them as image bearers of God no matter what their present situations. I recognized the need of people from the streets to come to a safe place, to be able to store their possessions, and to have routines, chores, responsibilities, and caring interactions with our staff and one another.

Practicing the Breakthrough of Presence

There are many ways to practice this breakthrough of presence. Just like we adopt spiritual disciplines to move us closer to Jesus through our times of prayer, Bible reading, and meditation, we can adopt disciplines that will bring us closer to the poor.

At Breakthrough, we invite people to just come and sit in our shelters, to share a meal, or to engage in meaningful conversation with our guests. Participating in the work of a ministry among the poor is a relatively safe way to learn about their experiences. We invite church groups to prepare and serve meals to our guests or to coach or tutor young people in the community through our sports and academic programs.

I know of many—myself included—who have taken trips to developing countries to widen our vision of the world and the needs of people who live in impoverished communities. Just go there, listen, and learn. You don't need an agenda. The Spirit will lead you to acts of service after you let your heart be broken by the needs of the poor. Transformation in the lives of the underprivileged starts first in our own transformation as we begin to see others through the loving eyes of God.

8

The Breakthrough of Being Spirit Led

One of the first things people ask when they are wrestling with how they should help the poor is "What should I do when someone asks me for money?" They are usually thinking of the many awkward times they have been hit up by a panhandler or even approached by a friend or someone else with a more substantial need. After hearing of panhandlers who collect hundreds of dollars a day in prime locations, perhaps they worry they would be enabling chronic begging if they respond with cash. Perhaps they suspect the one asking is putting on a show and faking the degree of need. Maybe the person will use the money for drugs or alcohol or in other foolish ways.

These are honest concerns. Before I respond, I need to set firmly in place my conviction that God actively leads us through his Holy Spirit

> *If you get the idea to do something good, just do it. It might be the Holy Spirit.*
>
> —Mary Stearns Sgarioto

if we will only listen and respond—and if we are not distracted by other "voices" that sometimes end up controlling our lives more than God.

Driven by Need

During an especially busy time when I had two preschoolers at home, I reached a crisis point. I was getting further and further behind in my work. The house was always a mess. I had stacks of papers everywhere. I was eating too much of all the wrong foods and feeding my young children crackers all day long. The laundry was never folded and put away. The kids learned they could find clean underwear in the clothes dryer amid wrinkled shirts and slacks. Time alone with God had become nonexistent.

In the height of my frenzy, I called a friend and began to unload my growing anxiety into her patient ear. "Arloa," she said when I finally stopped to take a breath, "I just finished reading something I think you need to hear. Consider this:

Never doubt. Have no fear. Watch the faintest tremor of fear, and stop all work, everything, and rest before Me until you are joyful and strong again . . . My work in the world has been hindered by work, work, work. Many a tireless, nervous body has driven a spirit. The spirit should be the master always, and just simply and naturally use the body as need should arise. Rest in Me.[1]

"Nothing is as important as the condition of your soul, Arloa," she warned. "I suggest you stop everything. Get away somewhere where you can be alone with God, where you will not be interrupted, and tell

God you will stay there until he is finished ministering to you. I've done that many times and he has never failed to meet me there."

That little admonition changed everything for me. I began to take notice when I felt my stomach tighten with stress. I welcomed my occasional bout of diverticulitis as a voice to me to step back, to say no, to focus on what God was calling me to do, rather than to rush ahead with my frenzied activities.

Those of us with hearts of compassion for the poor are especially prone to experience a disease called the "sacrifice syndrome." We are tempted to sacrifice our own needs and the needs of our families to meet the pressing needs of people around us. The complicated issues we face can become overwhelming. We feel driven to meet the needs of others. It is difficult to step away from our tasks and really listen to the voice of God. How do we respond in the face of such urgent need? How do we keep from running dry, from becoming tired, depressed, demanding, and cynical?

There was a period of time when many of us in our church in the city were experiencing several of the classic symptoms of the sacrifice syndrome. It was becoming increasingly difficult to navigate through the onslaught of conflict and controversy we were engaged in. All of us in leadership had been working hard to reach out to the broken and struggling members of our congregation and the wider community. I had led the charge to start Breakthrough Urban Ministries as an outreach of our church to the homeless men and women who were coming to the church offices during the week asking for handouts. The demands of the people were overwhelming.

There were so many needs, so much we felt we had to do, so many urgent projects to help our rapidly changing community. We started a food pantry, a tutoring ministry, ESL classes, GED classes, a new worship team, a small group ministry, a seniors' ministry, a prayer group for mothers of small children, and we were always available to anyone who called asking for counseling and prayer. All of these ministries were pressing and important, notwithstanding the myriad of basic survival needs we were trying to meet daily in our Breakthrough Center for the Homeless where we provided showers, food, clothing, and shelter for homeless men and women. Many of us were exhausted and beginning to get on one another's nerves. The church was in turmoil.

In an effort to make sense of the tempestuous waters swirling around us, we called on staff from Neil Anderson's Freedom in Christ ministry to guide us in a leadership retreat. Neil Anderson had just written a book called *Setting Your Church Free*, and he and his staff had developed a process to help churches that were stuck and couldn't seem to get free.

We gathered off site at the fellowship hall of another church and huddled in groups around easel pads and dry erase boards. We prayed and asked God to reveal to us what was causing such stress and dissension in our church.

After several hours of prayerful deliberation, God's message to us became clear: We had become consumed with meeting the overwhelming needs of everyone around us rather than listening quietly for the direction of the Holy Spirit and responding in joyful obedience to the direction of the Spirit of God. God's word to us that day was etched and underlined on one of our easel pads: "We must be led by the Spirit, rather than driven by need."

As we began to put that admonition into practice, we scaled back our activities and began to gather each morning in our little storefront room for prayer. Each day, we asked God to bring in the people whose lives needed the touch of the Holy Spirit, and we pledged ourselves to listen to the gentle nudge of the Spirit as we prayed, counseled, and cared for them. Soon, we began to experience what it meant to be led by the Spirit rather than driven by need.

Where the Spirit Leads

Once, in the early days of Breakthrough's ministry, I was getting ready to write payroll checks and realized we were going to be short on funds. I asked Judy Cuchetto if she could hold her check for a few days, and watched as dismay crept over her face. "I already wrote out my mortgage check," she said, clearly showing her stress. I didn't know what to do, but that day's mail brought a check for one thousand dollars, enough to get us through the tight spot.

Happily I called the elderly woman who had sent the check and told her how timely her gift had been and how we wouldn't have been able to pay our staff without it. She replied softly, "Sometimes the Spirit just leads me to do things like that." As Aletha had listened to God and obeyed the Spirit's prompting, God had used her at the exact moment we needed her gift.

Tony Evans, speaking at a Breakthrough retreat, retold the story of Abraham and his willingness to sacrifice Isaac. He reminded us that the ram that was caught in the bush had likely been there for some time, but no one had noticed. He said we often don't see God's provision until obedience is complete. As Abraham was obediently moving up the mountain to sacrifice the son whom he loved, God was already making provision for him!

One day, a large man walked into our Homeless Service Center and asked if we had a coat for him. It was freezing outside, and all he had to wear was a light, hooded sweatshirt. I went to look for a coat in our clothing room, but we didn't have a coat that would fit him. I was in the process of telling him, "I'm sorry, Billy, we don't have a coat that will fit you," when a man from our congregation came into the center with a big, beautiful down coat.

"This morning while I was praying, God led me to give you this coat," he said. "Can you use it?" Astonished, I took the coat from the donor and

The Breakthrough of Being Spirit Led

145

gave it to the homeless man and said, "Jesus really loves you, Billy!" Not only was I touched by the obvious love God was lavishing on this socially isolated and impoverished man, but I realized the man from our congregation was clearly being led by the Spirit. He had taken the time to listen to God in prayer that morning and had followed through with the gentle nudging to obey the instruction he had heard from God.

Listening to God and being prompted by the Spirit needs to be the basis for our action. God works in us and then out through us. In practical terms, this means we start our day in contemplation of God and God's Word. It means we spend time praying and listening for guidance before diving into action. It means we respond with obedience to those nudges of the Spirit when God instructs us to act. It is when we are moving in obedience that God can use us effectively to care for others.

The apostle Paul wrote, "The Lord is Spirit, and where the Spirit of the Lord is, there is freedom" (2 Cor. 3:17). Our actions of love for others may not be easy, but they are never a burden when we know we are doing what God calls us to do.

Where God Guides, God Provides

During one lean summer, Breakthrough ran out of money and food. By then, we were serving a hot lunch to nearly forty homeless men every day, as well as handing out groceries from our food pantry to low-income families in the neighborhood. Our cash had run so short that we couldn't even afford the three hundred dollars to fill our little truck with the groceries we could buy at the Greater Chicago Food Depository for a mere seven cents per pound.

As our staff gathered at the end of the day on a Friday, our Homeless Service Center director laid it all out: We would not be able to provide meals the following week! We joined hands and prayed, giving up our problem to God, asking for his provision, while resolving to only take each day as it came and offer whatever God provided.

At that time, our day center was not open on Saturdays. But on Sunday morning as I arrived at church for service, an usher met me at the door. "Have you seen the food pantry?" he asked.

"Yes, I know," I replied. "It's empty."

"Go look."

I opened the door and was shocked! The pantry was filled from floor to ceiling with post office boxes full of groceries! The usher worked for a suburban postal service, and the people at his work had collected groceries to feed hungry people. They didn't know about our need, and we didn't know about their collection. But when Bob, the usher, realized that the postal workers had collected more groceries than they were able to distribute to the programs on their list, he got permission and filled two vans full to stock our food pantry.

We served the men lunch and continued our food pantry distribution without missing a beat. I went to worship that day in awe of God's provision and love. Bob was a devoted follower of Jesus who listened to

Johnny

Johnny was a regular attender at our church. He would arrive late with his head down and go straight up the stairs to the balcony, where he could sit by himself so he would not have to talk to anyone. He usually carried a tattered grocery bag and a couple of newspapers. If I greeted him, he would look down, then hesitantly glance at me and say, "Oh, hi, Arloa," and then hurriedly walk away. If I met him on the street or in the park, he would go to great lengths to avoid me. I sometimes noticed him walking on the street, miles away from our church, always seeming to be in a hurry with his head down.

Sometimes he came to the church office during the week to talk about the Bible with Gary, our church administrator. Somehow he wasn't so shy in that setting. When we started Breakthrough, he ate with us occasionally, but he still preferred to spend his time in the church office with Gary talking about his favorite subject, the Word of God. He refused to stay in our shelter, preferring to walk miles to stay with relatives or under bridges. We were never really sure where he slept.

I have known Johnny for twenty years, and to my knowledge he is still walking the streets. He prefers to be alone.

the nudging of the Spirit and was used by God to bring in what we needed in great abundance.

We have seen many examples of this kind of provision through God's people over the years. Whenever we face a difficult situation, John Smith, our administrative director reminds us, "We have a history with God!" So we can trust that he will continue to provide through those who listen to the Spirit and obey.

A staff member closed the door of our center at the end of one day and remarked that we were out of deodorant. We would need to find the funds to buy deodorant for the forty homeless men who come to our shelter every day to eat and shower. Just then, there was a knock at the door. A woman entered with a Jewel (grocery store) bag. You guessed it! It was filled with deodorant.

A man was told he had a job he could start that very day, but he would need to wear brown pants. There were no brown pants in the clothing room, but that morning someone had donated a bag of clothes. In the bag was a pair of brown pants that fit him perfectly.

Later, when we opened a shelter for homeless women on the west side of Chicago, we continued to experience this amazing provision and love of God through letting the Spirit lead us. One day, we received a rather odd contribution. It was a medical exam table. Not really knowing why, we put the table in our storage room. The very next week a doctor came to us and asked if he could open a medical clinic for the women of our shelter. We moved the exam table into an empty office, and now doctors, nurse practitioners, and medical students come several times each week to provide medical services for our homeless women. God knew our need before we did and provided the exam table.

Late on a Saturday night, one of the staff members of our women's shelter took out the garbage, and to her dismay, the door handle fell off the door to the alley. The alley was known to be a place of dangerous activity. At that late hour on a weekend night, it was unlikely they could find someone to fix the door. The staff members were discussing who would sit by the alley door all night to ensure the safety of the thirty homeless women who would be sleeping inside, when the doorbell rang. At the door was a man unknown to the staff women on duty. The first words out of his mouth were, "Is there anything you need fixed around here?"

The man was a police officer friend of mine whose beat was in the vicinity of the shelter. As he was driving around in his squad car he felt led by the Spirit to come by the shelter and ask that question. He boarded up the door and came the next day to fix the handle.

Our employment coordinator secured a street cleaning contract that would nearly double our street cleaning business that provided transitional work opportunities for men with limited work history. He came back to the office and told another staff person that in order to adequately fulfill the contract, it would be very helpful to have another van to drive the workers to their job. Just then, a man we hadn't met before arrived at the door. He had a van outside that he wanted to donate to the ministry.

One time, Breakthrough staffers went online to find the best price for a suitcase needed by one of our shelter guests who would be taking the bus to start a new job at the Tyson chicken plant in Kansas. Just then a woman walked into the center toting a suitcase on wheels.

We have experienced time and time again the truth of the old adage "Where God guides, God provides." God doesn't just drop deodorant or suitcases out of the sky. He uses people like you and me, who listen and respond to the promptings of the Holy Spirit and are moved to action. He uses us to perform his miraculous work in the world.

My friend and mentor, Sibyl Towner, reminds me often that I always have enough time to do what God wants me to do. There is no need to rush, no need to worry. God will always supply what we need.

.

How Should We Respond to Panhandlers?

Taking time to listen to the still, small voice of God's Spirit is especially essential in trying to decide how to respond when someone we don't know asks us for money. Panhandlers seem to bombard us in the city. They wash our car windshields at the gas station and then come to our windows expecting payments. They cling to ragtag cardboard signs and approach us with forlorn faces. Some are in obvious need. We can tell by their faces that they truly are blind or they are missing legs or they are sitting in wheelchairs, holding dirty cups.

What should we do?

As the leader of a large organization that specializes in ministry among the homeless, let me give you my expert opinion: *I don't know!*

I think God gives us these dilemmas to cause us to rely on the compassion of Christ he has implanted in our hearts. Coming face-to-face with someone who asks us for money is an opportunity to be led by the Spirit instead of being driven by need, guilt, obligation, or the desire to bolster our own ego as a generous person. There is no simple answer.

Jesus said in Luke 6:30 that we are to give to everyone who asks of us. Most of us are hesitant to do that because we are afraid we will be taken advantage of. Perhaps the recipient of our charity will use our hard-earned cash for booze or drugs. Surely giving to someone who would use our money for those purposes would not be in anyone's best interest, would it? Yet, the directive is clear. We are to give without question and without judgment.

While we don't want to contribute to someone's addiction, it is helpful to understand that people who are living on the street usually do not have access to appropriate pain medicine, mental health counseling, or the gentle pacifiers such as chocolate and ice cream that we turn to when we need a lift. Who are we to judge them for how they spend money? I certainly have not always made the best decisions with the money God sends my way. Yet God keeps giving to me.

On the other hand, our gifts do not always have to be cash. I urge people to give their financial gifts to an organization like Breakthrough that specializes in wise care for the under-resourced and then get involved by volunteering to help the ministry. Then when asked for cash, we can then respond like Peter and John did when confronted by the crippled beggar. "Silver or gold I do not have, but what I have I give you. In the name of Jesus Christ of Nazareth, walk" (Acts 3:6).

A financial gift to a mission or an organization that provides opportunities for the homeless will help men and women who have been crippled by life get back on their feet and—in the name of Jesus Christ—walk a new walk. As stewards of the resources God entrusts to us, we want to make sure our gifts to the poor are invested wisely. I will address this more completely in the next chapter.

Instead of giving cash to people on the street, we can give directions, or perhaps a ride, to the nearest ministry that provides loving care in the name of Christ. Like the Good Samaritan Jesus described in Luke 10, we can transport those who are battered and broken to the nearest rehab center and pay for their rehabilitation.

I have a friend who always gives people exactly what they ask for. If they ask for change, he gives them change. If they ask for a couple of dollars, he gives them a couple of dollars. He says that in the grand scheme of things, considering his budget for giving to the poor, the amount of money he hands out is actually relatively small. He thinks we make a bigger deal of being taken advantage of than we should. After all, Jesus let himself be stripped, beaten, and hung on a cross unjustly to show his great love. It is not likely that we will ever experience that much injustice in our giving to the poor.

Oswald Chambers says, "Never make a principle out of your experience; let God be as original with other people as He is with you."[2] So, again, we are asked to let the Spirit guide our practices when we come face-to-face with someone asking us for money.

One thing I am quite certain about is this: When I stand before God in the judgment, I don't think God is going to drill me about how smart and frugal I was when faced with someone who asked me for money. I doubt God will point out how proud he is of me that I didn't let myself get scammed by someone who was lying to get a few bucks out of me.

God is more likely to say something like this:

I was hungry and you gave me something to eat, I was thirsty and you gave me something to drink, I was a stranger and you invited me in, I needed clothes and you clothed me, I was sick and you looked after me, I was in prison and you came to visit me . . . I tell you the truth, whatever you did for one of the least of these brothers of mine, you did for me. (Matt. 25:34–40)

Led to Pray

I don't even remember why I was so exhausted and depressed. I just know I went to bed with an oppressive foreboding that I couldn't shake. Everything in me ached. I struggled with my "dark night of the soul" until I fell into a fitful, anxiety-ridden sleep.

My alarm woke me the next morning in time to attend a 6:00 a.m. church prayer meeting. Instantly I knew something had changed. My heart was light and cheery. I bounced out of bed delighted to face the day. My heart sang with joy. I danced my happy self into the living room of one of our church members, where a small group of prayer warriors gathered.

"Arloa, are you all right?" asked Dorrine Kain. Dorrine's brother, Lester Foster, had been staying at her home while on furlough from his missionary work in Bolivia.

"Yes, I am great!" I responded. "Why do you ask?"

"My brother, Les, just returned from his two-hour prayer walk. He told me that for some reason this morning, God led him to pray for you, and he has been fervently interceding for you for the past two hours!"

I was dumbfounded. First of all, by the immense love God had for me, and secondly that Les Foster had made himself available to God at 4:00 a.m., which was his daily practice, and that he had been obedient to the call of God to pray for me. For two hours, while I slept, Les Foster was wrestling in the spirit world for my soul.

The following Sunday, I caught him at the door of our church. "Les, thank you so much for praying for me. You couldn't have known how important it was to me at that moment!"

He looked caringly into my grateful eyes and replied assuredly, "I know."

I wish I could tell you I have that kind of prayer life. I don't. People who sacrifice their precious sleep or relaxation time to pray for others know something about laying down their lives to follow Jesus. I hunger for that. Their obedience to the call of prayer effectively influences the deep spiritual work of pulling down strongholds and changing the course of our lives. The work of prayer is the most important work we can do. I know I need to be surrounded by people who know how to pray, and I need to prioritize my personal time with God above all.

Like those of us who tend to be excessively task-oriented, Jesus' disciples once "asked him, 'What must we do to do the works God requires?'

"Jesus answered, 'The work of God is this: to believe in the one he has sent'" (John 6:29). So simple, yet so profound. Genuinely believing is where all good works must start. To pray, to trust, to submit to God's lordship, to worship, to embrace God's priorities, and to believe that God is "able to do immeasurably more than all we ask or imagine, according to his power that is at work within us" (Eph. 3:20) is our necessary work that must supersede all other work.

The breakthrough of being Spirit led happens when we take time to wait upon and listen to God until we see what the Father is doing. Then we move joyfully in the Spirit to carry out God's work. By ourselves, we can do nothing.

The Breakthrough of Stewardship

9

Irving Wasserman was on a mission. His overarching concern in life was the national debt. He had a great mind for numbers and watched the interest rates and markets closely. He was sure that with wise economic policies and habits, he could personally make a difference, that if he lived frugally enough, he would be able to save money until the interest from the accumulated principal would offset our government spending. He had been mocked and shunned all his life, but he was determined to eradicate the national debt for his own self-respect.

> *Tell those rich in this world's wealth to quit being so full of themselves and so obsessed with money, which is here today and gone tomorrow. Tell them to go after God, who piles on all the riches we could ever manage—to do good, to be rich in helping others, to be extravagantly generous. If they do that, they'll build a treasure that will last, gaining life that is truly life.*
>
> —1 Timothy 6:17–19 (MSG)

I first saw Irving striding hurriedly past the Breakthrough Center for the Homeless shouting profanity at no one in particular. He was very odd looking. His legs were long and lanky and his clothing worn and dirty. The waistline of his pants was hiked up to his chest and the bottoms of his pant legs ended high above his ankles. A few days later, I saw him again peering through the storefront window.

"Would you like to come in for a cup of coffee?" I asked. He seemed pleased to be treated with respect and soon became one of our regular guests.

As Irving began to trust me, he told me he had been diagnosed with schizophrenia as a young man and was receiving a monthly disability check. He had been institutionalized for many years and had been given shock treatments. He spoke of being sexually assaulted in the state hospital and again out on the street after he was released. He was the object of frequent torment from neighborhood gangs. His quick pace and use of profanity were his only weapons of defense.

Clearly, Irving was very alone. Breakthrough became a family for him. He enjoyed talking about current events and the world economy. Sometimes he would make perfect sense; other times he would release a string of inflammatory accusations for no apparent reason, or become enraged over things that seemed insignificant. Conversations were unpredictable, but always interesting.

Irving was very particular about saving money. Once a year, he brought his dirty laundry to Breakthrough in a worn potato bag so he wouldn't have to put his quarters in a commercial washer at a Laundromat. He stuffed his pockets with used paper towels from the bathroom garbage to use for toilet paper at home so he could save money. He regularly ate at neighborhood churches and soup kitchens so he wouldn't have to buy groceries or use the gas to cook on his stove.

He lived by himself in a tiny basement apartment where the drain backed up sewage when it rained. The apartment hadn't been painted or renovated in years. Irving wanted it that way because he didn't want the landlord to raise the rent. He even asked us to help him move his stove out to the alley for the garbage men to pick up, because he didn't want to pay the monthly gas bill to keep the pilot light on.

He asked me if he could have his bank statements sent to my attention at Breakthrough in case something ever happened to him. Every month, we would review his statements. I soon began to notice a pattern of deposits for five cents or a quarter. When I questioned him about it, he told me he sometimes found loose change on the sidewalk and he would immediately deposit it at the local bank. "I can't trust myself with money," he'd say.

One Thanksgiving, I asked Irving to join our family for a traditional turkey dinner. Since I knew Irving was a diabetic, I picked up a package of sugar free ice cream sandwiches for his dessert. Irving ate the ice cream with great pleasure as the rest of us ate our pumpkin pie with whipped cream.

As our guests were preparing to leave, I handed Irving the rest of the ice cream sandwiches for him to take home. He accepted them gratefully.

The next morning Irving was banging at my door. He shoved the ice cream at me and growled, "Here, take these back. I can't eat them. They make me want to have them all the time."

Irving was determined not to let simple pleasures distract him from his goal.

One day, Irving walked into my office as I was finishing up a grant proposal to a community foundation. I was asking for support for our employment training program. "Listen to this, Irving," I said. "If we help someone get a job who has been receiving welfare, we save the government six thousand dollars a year in welfare benefits that would have been paid out, and in turn the newly employed worker will pay four thousand dollars in income taxes. That's a benefit of to the government of ten thousand dollars per year per person that we help employ, not to

Miss Martha

Miss Martha was missing. Her photo began to circulate in e-mails to homeless service providers throughout the city.

We were especially concerned for her because she had stayed with us for nearly a year. At eighty-four, Miss Martha was eligible for subsidized housing for seniors, but she felt more at home at Breakthrough and didn't want to leave. She certainly didn't want to lose her independence by going into a nursing home. Instead, she shuffled throughout our high-crime neighborhood, bent over and vulnerable, but happy to have found family.

Finally, we managed to convince Miss Martha to join her sister, her only known relative, at a local nursing home, and we said goodbye.

Now, just a few months later, we learned that Miss Martha's sister had passed away and Miss Martha had disappeared. Had she finally been mugged and left to a pauper's grave? Had someone kidnapped her for her Social Security checks? Was she lying wounded in a city hospital somewhere? No one knew.

Weeks dragged by until we got the news. Miss Martha had been found. She had cashed her check at a currency exchange and caught a bus to Florida where she was living in another shelter, stubbornly independent and free.

mention the savings if the worker is receiving employer health benefits instead of relying on government-supported healthcare."

Irving reviewed my numbers with clear interest. I could tell his mathematical mind was projecting the savings over multiple years and multiple employees.

A few days later, Irving asked me to help him find a lawyer who would set up a revocable living trust for his estate. Someone who would not require him to pay for their services! He said he knew he didn't have long to live and that he had decided he wanted to give his savings to Breakthrough to be used for job training for the homeless and mentally ill. A year later, Irving was hospitalized with terminal cancer and hepatitis C, and he died shortly thereafter.

By living frugally Irving had saved seven hundred dollars per month from his disability checks and had purchased government bonds every quarter for fifty years. With his gift to Breakthrough of five hundred thousand dollars, this eccentric man, who had been forgotten by many, became our largest donor. His legacy has lived on through the changed lives of people who have been trained and employed because of his gift.

Irving was one of the many examples I have seen of the way God uses people whom the world considers to be weak and foolish to confound the wise (1 Cor. 1:27). At Breakthrough, we work hard to acquire and cultivate donors to support the ministry, yet Irving, who would curse and drool and in every way appeared to be indigent, was able to contribute financially in a way no other individual has.

Certainly, most of us are not going to live like Irving did. But I have learned many great lessons about stewardship from this simple man.

Stewards, Not Owners

"It's not my money!" Irving would insist. As a result of his lifelong mental disability, Irving was unable to work and therefore didn't feel he had earned his money. He was just a steward of it, and he was intent on investing it so it would do the most for the common good. A steward is a person who takes care of someone else's property.

In fact, we are all simply caretakers of what God has entrusted to us. God is the maker and rightful owner of everything. "I have no need of a bull from your stall or of goats from your pens," said the Lord, "for every animal of the forest is mine, and the cattle on a thousand hills" (Ps. 50:9–10). David declared, "The earth is the LORD's, and everything in it, the world, and all who live in it" (Ps. 24:1).

God owns everything but trusts us to manage creation as caretakers. In Genesis, God gave Adam and Eve instructions to care for the earth, to subdue it, and to rule over it (Gen. 1:28). God owned the garden. They were the caretakers. When the Israelites were poised to enter the Promised Land, they were reminded that the land belonged to God (Deut. 11:12). They were temporary tenants.

The concept of stewardship continues in the New Testament in the parables of Jesus. On several occasions, Jesus spoke of a master or owner who entrusted resources to a caretaker. Upon the owner's return, the stewards were either commended or chastised depending upon how well they had managed what had been entrusted to them. (See Luke 12:42–48; 16:1–13; 19:12–27; Matt. 25:14–20.) What mattered was not how much they were given, but what they did with the resources that had been entrusted into their care.

If God owns everything, why does it seem that some people have so much and others so little? Well, because we worked hard for it, right? Did you ever stop to wonder what your life would be like if you were born in a remote village in Africa, or in an inner-city neighborhood where there was limited access to education or economic opportunities? Indeed, even our ability to produce wealth comes from God (Deut. 8:18). If we are honest with ourselves, we have to admit that everything we have—our work ethic, our talents, our education, our network of support, everything—is a gift (James 1:17).

Wise Investments

Though Irving was mentally ill, he recognized the need to invest wisely. When friends of the ministry heard he had invested in government bonds during the seventies, eighties, and nineties, when the stock market was booming, many shook their heads. If only he would have put the money in stocks or a good mutual fund, he could have built even greater wealth.

I knew why Irving bought government bonds. His checks came every month from the government, so he invested in the government that was providing for him. In Irving's mind, even his investments did not belong to him. He trusted in the source of the resources, which in his mind was the U.S. Government, and he was committed to build interest through government bonds and give it back to the government.

Jesus tells the story of a man who gave ten of his servants one mina each, the equivalent of three months' wages, and instructed them to "put the money to work" while he was away. When he came back from his journey, the master sent for the servants to whom he had given the money "to find out what they had gained with it" (Luke 19:12–27).

One of the servants had wisely invested the money and had gotten a tenfold return. Let's say in today's terms the servant was given twelve thousand dollars (three months' wages on a forty-eight thousand dollars per year salary). When the master returned from his journey, this faithful servant had turned that money into one hundred twenty thousand dollars. You can imagine the delight of the master. He calls him good, and probably pats him on the back as he says, "Well done!"

Another servant holds up his puny mina and says proudly, "Sir, here is your mina; I have kept it laid away in a piece of cloth. I was afraid of you, because you are a hard man. You take out what you did not put in and reap what you did not sow."

You can imagine the dismay of the master, especially when you realize that Jesus is teaching about our responsibility to be good stewards of what has been given to us by our Master. Clearly the foolish servant didn't know the expectations of the master. The master had instructed him to "put this money to work." Instead, he acted in fear and clung tightly to what he had been given.

The master was not pleased. He called the servant "wicked" and told him his own words would judge him. He took the mina from the wicked servant and gave it to the wise one.

Like the servants in the story, God entrusted us with various gifts and talents. We are responsible, for a period of time, to put them to work, to invest them, to bring a return. Certainly we need to use the resources that come our way to provide food, clothing, and shelter for our families, but decisions about what we spend and how we invest should always be carefully considered in light of how they will bring the greatest return for the kingdom of God, for the owner of all that we are and have.

Irving was a very simple man who recognized that he was not the owner of what he had and that he needed to make wise investments. Ultimately, he recognized that investing in the work of caring Christians who were putting people to work who would otherwise be locked in their addiction, isolation, and poverty was the ultimate best use of his resources.

If we take seriously the words of Scripture, we will want to do all we can to make a difference in the lives of hurting people through our wise investments as well. With just fifteen thousand dollars, we can drill a well in Zambia through Living Water International or World Vision that will provide clean water to thousands of people.[1] You can join a group of others who are sponsoring clean water. The ROI (return on investment) is staggering; lives are saved, and children and their families are able to participate in education and industry during the time they otherwise would have spent walking for miles to access water.

Investments in groups such as the International Justice Mission will help to rescue women and children from the evils of human trafficking, saving countless men and women from the devastating abuse of sexual exploitation. How can we measure the ROI on such a meaningful investment?

Volunteering our talents at tutoring or cooking will make lives more meaningful for the homeless and for children in underprivileged communities in our cities. Contributions that provide food, shelter, and clothing for the homeless population in America are investments that change lives both now and forever. These investments in the people God loves are investments that will last for eternity. Together we can make a real difference in the lives of those Jesus called, "the least of these," and in the process, we get to experience the joy of giving back to the One who has given us all things.

We need lots of creative thought to meet the challenges of caring for the poor in America. Business creation and incentives, entrepreneurship, micro-enterprise, real estate development, urban farming, creation of affordable housing, legislation that will defend the rights of the poor—all of these and more are areas in which those who have special skills can be free to experiment, discover, and develop new ideas.

As U2 lead singer Bono says, "This is not a burden. This is an adventure. Don't let anyone tell you it cannot be done. We can be the generation that ends extreme poverty."[2] Our investments in bringing people into God's love are investments that will compound exponentially and will last forever. All of us, working together, investing the gifts God has given us, can make a lasting impact in the world and in the lives of people that will last forever.

Self-Denial

"Here, take this. I can't have them," Irving insisted, handing back the ice cream sandwiches I had given him. "They make me want to have them all the time." Irving didn't want to jeopardize his mission to change the world by allowing himself to become enslaved by material things. He was willing to sacrifice his own pleasure for a greater purpose.

What is your life purpose? What is the legacy you want to leave after you're gone?

I have been inspired by many generous givers who, like Irving, have been willing to make personal sacrifices in order to invest resources into kingdom work. When my brother, Doug, enrolled at LeTourneau University in Texas, I heard the story of R. G. LeTourneau, who built wealth through the invention and manufacture of earth-moving equipment. Recognizing his success was a gift to be used for the kingdom, he contributed 90 percent of his wealth to Christian endeavors. LeTourneau lived by the statement, "If you're not serving the Lord, it proves you don't love him; if you don't love him, it proves you don't know him."[3]

Dr. Stanley Tam, the founder of U.S. Plastics, decided to live on a moderate salary and gave his entire business to God. At age twenty, Tam had an idea and started his own business. In 1936, on the road trying to sell his idea, he ran out of money. "I was stranded and broke except for thirteen cents and two gallons of gas."

"God," he prayed, "what shall I do?"

"Start for home. I'll see that you get there," is the answer Tam received. He accepted the challenge and started to head toward home. He spent his last thirteen cents—a nickel on a hamburger and eight cents on gas (this was 1936, after all).

As his gas was running out, he felt led to pick up a hitchhiker. The stranger turned out to be a farmer in need of a ride, and he paid for the rest of Stanley's gas to get home.

Tam never forgot that God sends strangers along our paths to meet our needs if we will step out and obey God.

As his business grew, Tam made God his formal business partner and committed 51 percent of the business profits to Christian ministry. Years later as his business continued to succeed, he heard the Lord ask him, "Would you be willing to turn your entire business over to me?"

Believing God wanted to convert his earthly wealth into eternal treasures, he said, "Thank you, Lord. You can have it all."

Since then, Dr. Tam has given millions to kingdom work. Now in his nineties, Dr. Tam still travels to share his financial testimony.[4]

I have personally been inspired and challenged by the faithfulness of so many people who donate to Breakthrough as I have watched them put real faith into action. One of our donors who was significantly impacted by the recession of 2008 wrote:

I have been studying Elisha and the story of the man in 2 Kings 4:42–44 who brought twenty loaves to Elisha. It was probably his tithe, and Elisha was able to feed the one hundred people with him, and there were leftovers!—during a famine! Don't you love God? He can take even a small amount of money and make it go farther than we ever dreamed it would go!

Here's another note that came with a large unexpected donation:

We have certainly been impacted by the financial decline in 2008 (of course that doesn't make us special!), but we continue to be challenged by God to give generously and faithfully. We have been meditating on the story in Mark of the "Young Rich Man" and have been following Jesus' simple and clear words: "You have only one thing left to do . . . sell your possessions, give to the poor and follow me."

"Only one thing left to do" is the mantra we are focusing on when we are worried about the scarcity of money and want to keep it for ourselves—it is encouraging us to give.

Another of our supporters decided to restrict herself to 176 dollars per month for groceries, which is what Illinois Food Stamp recipients receive, so she can continue to give during the recession.[5] She is practicing what she calls "intentional self-regulation."

Self-regulation is not a practice most would use to describe American Christians in the twenty-first century. Indeed, we live in an age of unprecedented consumerism and self-indulgence. The public storage industry is booming as we Americans buy more space to store all of the stuff we own. We have bigger houses, drive more cars, and eat out more often than ever.

Emerson, Smith, and Snell, in their book *Passing the Plate: Why American Christians Don't Give Away More Money*, write:

> Materialistic consumption has become a nearly inescapable way of life in the United States . . . the dominance of mass consumerism works powerfully and in many ways against American Christians freely and liberally giving away significant proportions of their incomes to people, ministries, needs, and good causes, as most of their religious traditions call them to do. The first and perhaps most formidable rival to generous voluntary financial giving of American Christians, then, aiding and abetting any of their natural human tendencies toward selfishness and stinginess, is America's institutionalized mass consumerism.[6]

We have allowed our mass-consumerism economy to lock us into commitments that consume most of our income. "It is not that they do not actually have the annual incomes to give generously," write Emerson, Smith, and Snell. "It is rather that they have already made and continue to make long-term household and consumer purchase decisions that commit most of their money to be spent in ways that leave little left over to give away."[7] Their studies actually revealed that the more income we make, the more we tend to become stingy, protective, and distrustful.[8]

We have become so imprisoned by our addiction to market consumerism that together American Christians give away less than 2 percent of our income to any kind of charity.[9] Many of us actually think we are poor, even though we have incomes that are in the top percentiles of the world. Just as God wants to free impoverished urban dwellers from economic and social poverty and isolation, God wants to free those of us with relative wealth and substantial income from our ghetto of self-indulgence.

As I write this book, America and the world are in the grips of a recession that is touching nearly all of our lives. Compounded greed and self-indulgence has threatened the collapse of our economic system. Today, as never before, we are being called to take a fresh look at what is important to us and to make adjustments in our lifestyles that will free us from our dependence upon material things.

There are basic principles that we can put into practice to experience the breakthrough of stewardship. One is to give away the first 10 percent. I was amused by the response of one of the people interviewed by Emerson, Smith, and Snell in their book. He said, "I would give 10 percent if I had it!"[10] If we believe the Bible calls us to tithe, then according to those same Scriptures, we are called upon to give the first 10 percent, not the last. We give the firstfruits of our labor.

We Need a Plan

Emerson, Smith, and Snell discovered themes of planning, deliberation, prioritizing, and routine were consistent in their interviews with generous givers. Those who work their giving into a well-planned budget are able to resist the captivity of American consumerism. They give routinely and regularly through disciplined habits and thoughtful practices.

The first step might be to assess our tax return and determine what percentage of our income we are presently contributing to charity and then set a goal to increase that percentage by 1 percent each year until we reach the 10 percent tithing goal and beyond. Emerson, Smith, and Snell have discovered that if 90 percent of committed Christian households in the United States would give away 10 percent of their after tax income, we could raise 85.5 billion dollars each year above what is currently given. What a difference this could make in meeting the needs of the poor![11] The sad fact is that one in five Christians in the U.S. give literally nothing to church, para-church, or nonreligious charities![12]

Those of us who are encumbered by consumer debt, who have mortgaged our homes to buy stuff, can benefit from listening to Dave Ramsey.[13] Dave celebrates those who have disciplined themselves to get out of debt. His advice? "Sell so much stuff the kids think they're next. Name the dog Ebay!" He says there are five basic things that will change your life: live on less than you make, get out of debt, create a budget, save for a rainy day, and give, give, give. "You were made to be a giver," says Ramsey. "It's in your DNA. When you give, it turns loose passion and creativity in your life."[14] Our bondage to bank debts and credit cards is hindering us from being good and faithful stewards and from experiencing the wonderful joy of giving.

Is It Okay that I'm Wealthy?

Those of us who live and work in areas of great poverty can become a bit jaded toward people with money. Yet throughout Scripture, we read of men and women who were entrusted with wealth.

Zacchaeus was a wealthy man. He had learned how to use the system for his own benefit. When he put his faith in Jesus, it changed not only his heart, but the way he used his money. He recognized immediately that those he had cheated needed to be repaid four times as much, and he pledged to give half of all he owned to the poor (Luke 10:1–10).

Mary, Martha, and Lazarus lived in Bethany, a Jerusalem "burb" described as "remarkably beautiful, the perfection of retirement and repose, of seclusion and lovely peace."[15] This was a town to which Jesus often retired, especially to the home of his dearest friends: Mary, Martha, and Lazarus. (See Matt. 21:17; 26:6; Mark 11:11; 14:3; Luke 24:50; John 11:1; 12:1.) Their home was spacious enough to accommodate a "great crowd" at a dinner given in Jesus' honor (John 12:12). So it seems they were people of means who were using their wealth for the kingdom in such a freehanded way that there is nothing recorded in Scripture of Jesus telling them they needed to divest themselves of their assets.

Joseph of Arimathea was a prominent member of the Council who had not consented to the crucifixion. He was a rich man, and Luke described him as a "good and upright" man. He was so financially secure that he had prepaid his own funeral. He was moved to donate his tomb to Jesus. (See Matt. 27:57–61; Mark 15:32–46; Luke 23:5–53.)

Several passages in the Gospels mention a group of women who followed Jesus and supported his work "out of their own means." They cared for his needs and assisted with his burial by donating their own spices and perfumes. (See Luke 8:1–3; 23:55—24:10; Mark 15:40; 16:1.)

We are not all called to take an oath of poverty, but we are called to be obedient. Some of us might be asked to take radical steps. Jesus told the rich young man to sell everything he had and give it to the poor. The man's face fell, and he went away sad. This may have been a test of his heart, for later Jesus said, "How hard it is for the rich to enter the kingdom of God!" (Mark 10:23). Jesus knew that the rich young man had a "god" he put above the God of heaven. He was not able to release his wealth, even to receive eternal life.

Riches can be a distraction from God's purposes or a means to achieve God's purposes, depending upon our hearts and callings. Those who are called by God to create wealth and invest in the kingdom should do so with gusto, using every bit of their financial wisdom to create wealth and to make wise kingdom investments.

Giving is similar to fasting. It releases us from our preoccupation with material things and allows us focus on what matters. It removes the illusion that we are self-sufficient and frees us to depend on God, who richly supplies us with all we need. Jesus said, "You Pharisees clean the outside of the cup and dish, but inside you are full of greed and wickedness . . . Give what is inside the dish to the poor, and everything will be clean for you" (Luke 11:39–41).

Those of us who have been given the ability to create wealth have a special responsibility to invest wisely and to put those resources to work. We do this by listening to God's call on our hearts. There is a reciprocal relationship between our treasure and our hearts. Jesus said, "Where your treasure is, there your heart will be also" (Matt. 6:21). Our hearts will follow our investments and our investments will follow our hearts. Once you start to give, you will find great joy in giving. Your heart will become soft and your love will increase. Generous giving is good for us.

I never apologize for asking people to give to the ministry of Breakthrough because I have seen people experience great joy as they have watched their investments grow in the lives of the men, women, and children who are transformed by the ministry. We don't have cranky givers. As the apostle Paul wrote, "Each . . . should give what he has decided in his heart to give, not reluctantly or under compulsion, for God loves a cheerful giver" (2 Cor. 9:7).

Teaching Stewardship to Our Children

When we live lives of economic indulgence, we tend to pass that habit on to our children. By indulging their desire for the latest gadgets, we may actually be teaching them consumerist habits that will keep them trapped for the rest of their lives. We can get in the way of the work of God in their lives by rushing in to rescue them from situations God has designed to make them stronger. They don't need to depend upon God, they have us.

I have been inspired by families who have made it a practice to serve together at our homeless shelters or have taken trips together to developing countries where their children come face-to-face with the poor. Some have included their children in funding decisions in their charitable donations. As the children have grown older, they have volunteered to tutor in our after-school program or coach a baseball or basketball team.

Several young girls in a Chicago suburb formed a club called The Gift Givers Club. They sponsored a lemonade stand, a garage sale, and a race to raise money to support Breakthrough's Youth and Family Program. One young girl who had a heart for the homeless asked to be given blankets instead of gifts one Christmas. She brought the blanket gifts to our homeless shelter. Another girl organized a trip with her friends to Chicago to hand out scarves and gloves to the homeless. These are children and young people who are being challenged by the adults in their lives to invest their time, talents, and treasure in the kingdom. They are experiencing the breakthrough of stewardship, developing giving habits that will likely stay with them for life.

The Breakthrough of Discipline

One of my favorite movies is the first *Rocky* movie. Rocky, a small-time boxer, is given the opportunity of a lifetime. In a publicity stunt, Rocky is asked to fight the heavyweight champion of the world, Apollo Creed. Clearly the underdog, Rocky begins to train under his old coach, Mickey.

The music swells as Rocky does one-armed pushups and runs throughout the city of Philadelphia, first alone, and later joined by throngs of runners inspired by his dedication and discipline. His girlfriend's brother, Paulie, works at a meat locker and lets Rocky punch the carcasses hanging in the freezers. Rocky exchanges his normal eating habits for raw-egg shakes, anything that will build his strength and prepare him for what lies ahead.

> *The spirit of the disciplines is nothing but the love of Jesus, with its resolute will to be like him whom we love.*
>
> —Dallas Willard

Finally, on the evening before the match, Rocky is walking with his girlfriend, Adrian. He is nervous about the fight and declares, "Adrian, all I wanna do is go da distance."

The scene flashes to the ring, and we watch as round after round, Rocky takes a brutal beating. His face is badly bruised, and his eye has to be opened by his trainer so he can see. To the amazement of the crowd, Rocky, determined to "go da distance," stays in the fight, round after round after round.

The bell rings for the final round. No one has expected him to get this far. Exhausted, Rocky takes a hit that lands him spread eagle on the mat. The screaming crowd rises to their feet as Rocky struggles to get up. Mickey, his coach, yells, "Stay down, Rocky. You've fought a good fight. Stay down!"

But Rocky is committed to "go da distance." He pulls himself up on the first rope. "Stay down," Mickey yells. "You don't have to fight anymore. Stay down!"

Ignoring this advice, Rocky pulls himself up on the ropes and staggers to his feet. The bell rings and Rocky is ecstatic. Even though he didn't win the fight, he accomplished what he set out to do. He went the distance.

While we may not be training for a heavyweight boxing match, most of us have incorporated some disciplines into our daily routine. We try to eat healthy foods; we brush our teeth; we go to work every day; we do the dishes; and we fold the laundry. Some of us even exercise regularly. If we want to obtain a university degree, we discipline ourselves to read and study while others are playing. We set goals and work hard to achieve the things that are meaningful to us.

Eventually these disciplines become habits. Our habits determine whether we live the lives we want to live. We prioritize our activities so that our behaviors develop us into the people we want to be.

A Different Kind of Fast

Many of us who desire to follow Jesus and imitate the way he lived have decided at some point to place spiritual disciplines into our lives. We do this because we want to grow in our relationship with the Lord. Spiritual disciplines help us grow spiritually. We fast, pray, meditate, read our Bibles, meet in small groups with other Christians, and go to church. These important disciplines keep us spiritually healthy. Without regular time set aside to focus on God, and to read and meditate on the Word, we tend to get off track spiritually and lose sight of God's work in the world and in us.

According to the Lord, the people in Isaiah 58 were doing many of the things we typically expect disciplined Christians to do, but they were frustrated in their efforts. God seemed far away and unresponsive to their prayers.

The Lord laid out another set of disciplines that would bring them into right relationship with God and with others:

Is not this the kind of fasting I have chosen: to loose the chains of injustice and untie the cords of the yoke, to set the oppressed free and break every yoke? Is it not to share your food with the hungry and to provide the poor wanderer with shelter—when you see the naked, to clothe him, and not to turn away from your own flesh and blood? Then your light will break forth like the dawn, and your healing will quickly appear; then your righteousness will go before you, and the glory of the LORD will be your rear guard. Then you will call, and the LORD will answer; you will cry for help, and he will say: Here am I. If you do away with the yoke of oppression, with the pointing finger and malicious talk, and if you spend yourselves in behalf of the hungry and satisfy the needs of the oppressed, then your light will rise in the darkness, and your night will become like the noonday. The LORD will guide you always; he will satisfy your needs in a sun-scorched land and will strengthen your frame. You will be like a well-watered garden, like a spring whose waters never fail. (Isa. 58:6–11)

The people the Lord was addressing in this passage missed a discipline that was central to their quest to know God. They were not caring for the poor. I have rarely heard of caring for the poor as a spiritual discipline, yet it seems to me, according to passages of Scripture like this one and Matthew 25, where Jesus speaks of caring for the needy as if we were caring for him, that this is a discipline that needs central focus in our Christian tradition and practice. In our individualistic approach to growing as Christians, we may very well be missing a vitally important key to our spiritual development.

By incorporating disciplines that include feeding the hungry and providing the poor wanderer with shelter, we experience the Lord's light, strength, provision, and guidance. Isaiah 58 is strangely silent about the effects of such actions upon the recipients of such kindness. Instead, caring for the physical and social needs of the impoverished is identified as acts of worship to God, and then, as a result, we experience God. We become like well-watered gardens and receive our own healing.

What practices have you incorporated into your life that draw you close to God? Do they include caring for the poor? What would it look like if you reordered your life to include care for the broken and impoverished as one of your spiritual disciplines?

Training for the Race

Physical exercise is a good way to illustrate discipline. In fact, the apostle Paul used it in just such a way. "Do you not know that in a race all the runners run, but only one gets the prize? Run in such a way as to get the prize. Everyone who competes in the games goes into strict training. They do it to get a crown that will not last; but we do it to get a crown that will last forever" (1 Cor. 9:24–25).

Like Sylvester Stallone's character in *Rocky*, the apostle Paul had determined he needed to discipline himself. His desire to go the distance meant he needed to put himself under strict training.

In the spring of 2007, I made the decision to run a marathon. At the time, I was not exercising regularly and was not at all ready to complete a 26.2-mile race. Determined to go the distance, I downloaded a training schedule and began to follow it religiously.

Fortunately for me, my training didn't start with long runs. I started walking and running short distances and then gradually progressed until I was running ten to twelve miles every weekend. It took lots of time and dedication. Many mornings, running thirteen or fourteen times around the Garfield Park Lagoon was the last thing I wanted to do. But I had made a public decision, and I knew I needed to train if I wanted to accomplish my goal. When I didn't feel like running, I would convince myself to at least put on my running shoes. Getting started was often the hardest part. Little by little, I grew in my ability to run longer distances.

As it turns out, I happened to choose the only Chicago marathon that was halted at the halfway point because of extreme heat. Despite many admonitions from race officials to stop, I was one of the fortunate ones who managed to complete the race. If I had not made the decision in advance to "go the distance," and if I hadn't trained diligently, I would have stopped long before the finish line when I felt pain and exhaustion.

The discipline of training ourselves in care for the poor similarly starts with a decision and with small steps.

Nourish Your Relationship with the Lord

Since 1985, I have made it my practice to read the Bible completely through every year. Because of this constant intake of Scripture, the Spirit often uses passages of the Bible to speak into situations in my life and to move me toward action.

I also spend time in the slower reading of Scripture, prayer, meditation, and reflection. I have a space in the study of my little apartment that is set aside for this purpose. I light a few candles to symbolize the light of Christ and to mark my focus on sitting in God's presence. I read Scripture passages and meditations from the Upper Room *Guide to Prayer* and sit quietly with God, listening to the word that God has for me for the day.[1]

The disciplines of prayer and Scripture meditation often lead me to acts of service that I might not otherwise have considered. When Dr. Yonggi Cho, pastor of the eight-hundred-fifty-thousand-member Yoido Full Gospel Church in Seoul, Korea, was asked how his church grew, he remarked, "We pray, and we obey." In prayer, we learn what God is doing so we can move forward in obedience to his will. This dynamic combination empowers us do God's work on the earth in God's way.

Find Your Place

With a little research you will discover that there are organizations and ministries in your community that feed and shelter the homeless, build houses, settle refugees, mentor and tutor youth, teach English as a second language, assist young women with unplanned pregnancies, visit people in prisons, nursing homes, and hospitals, and similar activities. So, what is your passion area? Frederick Buechner says, "The place God calls you to is the place where your deep gladness and the world's deep hunger meet."[2]

Your place could be anywhere. I know a bank president who maintains vehicles at a shelter, a therapist who visits women in prison, a financial consultant who volunteers at a shelter, a marketing executive who leads twelve-step recovery groups, a business executive who coaches baseball in an inner-city sports league, a retiree who visits people in a nursing home, a landscape designer who tutors kids every week with her daughter, a retired executive whose family is helping to settle an African refugee family, and a hair stylist who does art projects with kids at an inner-city youth organization.

Serving moved these men and women outside the comfort of their sanitized environments and brought them face-to-face with Jesus in his distressing disguise where they received more than they were able to give.

You might begin by visiting organizations that interest you. Begin donating to causes that touch your heart in some way or that you wish touched your heart. Your passion will grow as you get involved. Ask what is needed and how you can help. You will soon discover there is no shortage of opportunities to impact the lives of hurting people.

Consult Guides Who Are Further Along

When I started Breakthrough, I sought out mentors who were already caring for people in areas of need in the city. I asked them lots of questions. I found help from members of the Christian Community Development Association (CCDA) and began attending the annual CCDA conference that brings together practitioners who are working in many of the forgotten places of the world. They helped me form a training plan, to learn how to care for people without enabling them, to stay focused on mission.

Serving those who cannot reciprocate activates our faith and stretches our capacity to love. Jesus said, "If you love those who love you, what reward will you get? Are not even the tax collectors doing that? And if you greet only your brothers, what are you doing more than others? Do not even pagans do that?" (Matt. 5:46–47).

The more we love God, the more we will love people. The higher and deeper we go with God, the wider our hearts and hands will reach out to those around us. But love is reciprocal: The more we love people, the more we will love God.

Avoiding Legalism

Throughout my life, I have struggled with legalism. To be disciplined without being legalistic about it is a challenge for me. There are so many "oughts." I ought to pray and read my Bible every day. I ought to exercise. And now, another: I ought to serve the poor. Over and over again, I fall short of what I think I ought to be doing. The apostle Paul wrote about a similar frustration in Romans 7: "What I want to do I do not do, but what I hate I do. And if I do what I do not want to do . . . For I have the desire to do what is good, but I cannot carry it out" (Rom. 7:15–16, 18).

The inner battle left Paul feeling wrecked: "What a wretched man I am! Who will rescue me from this body of death?" (Rom. 7:24). He immediately answered his own question: "Thanks be to God—through Jesus Christ our Lord! . . . Therefore, there is now no condemnation for those who are in Christ Jesus, because through Christ Jesus the law of the Spirit of life set me free from the law of sin and death" (Rom. 7:25—8:2).

If God no longer condemns us, then certainly we do not need to condemn ourselves. God has forgiven us through the blood of Christ. Not only are we forgiven for the times when we have broken our covenant with God, but we are also forgiven for our transgressions against others. We are forgiven for buying coffee that is not fair traded, for eating tacos whose companies have oppressed tomato pickers, for wearing shirts and shoes that have been made by impoverished workers in sweatshops. Thank God, we are forgiven.

Yet, because of our love for God and people, we will do all we can to live in such a way that our actions will not cause others to suffer. We don't do it out of guilt or obligation but out of love. God loved us first. Jesus demonstrated how to love by laying down his life for us. We follow Christ by laying down our lives for one another, by loving and serving one another, by washing one another's feet. The apostle Paul said, "The only thing that counts is faith expressing itself through love" (Gal. 5:6). We buy fair-trade coffee because we love the coffee pickers.

Mrs. No

"Pastor, you have to do something about that woman!" The church chairman pointed his angry finger in my husband's face and let him have it. He and his group of friends who regularly journeyed into the city for services from the suburbs represented the "old guard" of the church. It was their ancestors who had founded the church one hundred ten years ago, and they were not about to let their high standards for traditional worship be violated by "that woman" who sat every Sunday in the very front row with arms outstretched in unwavering adoration.

Mrs. No bellowed out her praise louder than anyone in the congregation, slightly off key and consistently two beats ahead of everyone else. And she distracted the properly dressed congregates with her multi-layered, gaudy, long dresses, clunky plastic jewelry, and the red lipstick she spread unevenly across the entire front of her face.

My husband agreed to "have a talk" with Mrs. No. He worked out a deal with her that if she would just sit quietly during the singing of the hymns, he would reward her with extra food from the food pantry. It worked for a Sunday or two, and then Mrs. No simply disappeared, never to bother—or bless—us again.

Painful, but Worth It

Discipline is not easy. It involves getting up off the couch and turning off mindless television programs. It might mean doing things that are difficult for us, that stretch us. It involves making plans that cause us to put aside personal comfort and venture into the unknown, into places that make us uncomfortable, places that might include risk and pain. It involves making bold plans and taking courageous steps.

The writer of Hebrews said:

> Therefore, since we are surrounded by such a great cloud of witnesses, let us throw off everything that hinders and the sin that so easily entangles, and let us run with perseverance the race marked out for us. Let us fix our eyes on Jesus, the author and perfecter of our faith, who for the joy set before him endured the cross, scorning its shame, and sat down at the right hand of the throne of God . . . No discipline seems pleasant at the time, but painful. Later on, however, it produces a harvest of righteousness and peace for those who have been trained by it. Therefore, strengthen your feeble arms and weak knees. (Heb. 12:1–2, 11–12)

Jesus was able to endure the painful discipline of the cross because of the joyous anticipation of rising victorious and redeeming the world to God; expressing love to the lonely, the oppressed, and the captives, and unleashing the Spirit of God on the earth so his followers could do even greater things than he did (John 14:12). Joy comes when we practice the discipline of engaging regularly with those who are less fortunate. We, too, can persist in our discipline because of the joy set before us.

Like after a good run, we experience many positive results when we discipline ourselves to care for the poor. We are inspired by true heroes who are making the most of their circumstances and succeeding against all odds. We experience the flow of the power and love of God through us as we let God use us to encourage the oppressed and as we join them in their struggle. We get to watch as God transforms the lives of men and women as they enter into the loving community of faith, those who for the first time in their lives experience healing and new life through Christ's love. Our discipline produces a harvest of righteousness and peace as we put our faith into action because of our love for God and people. We experience God when we get near the brokenhearted. Our lives become well-watered gardens and our springs never fail.

The nights I go with friends to serve dinner and sing hymns with the women in Breakthrough's homeless shelter, I almost always have to push through a wave of negative thoughts of "I don't want to go tonight," but inevitably, when the night is over and I am on my way home, I am so happy that I pushed through to get there. I always leave inspired and uplifted. I receive so much more than I can ever give.

Like Rocky, it all starts with the decision to go the distance and to put ourselves into strict training so that we push through to the finish, so that we can experience the flow of God's love through us to others. This is the joy of the breakthrough of discipline.

The Breakthrough of Joining a Movement

"This little light of mine, I'm gonna let it shine." As a child, I loved that song. I held my finger proudly in the air, circling it above my head. I would let my little candle glow brightly until Jesus came. I wouldn't let Satan snuff it out. I was "gonna let it shine, let it shine, let it shine." I was personally going to make a difference in the world by letting my little light shine brightly. I sang with childlike determination.

It wasn't until later that I learned when Jesus said we are to let our lights so shine before men that they may see our good deeds and glorify the Father in heaven, he used a plural tense. Since

> *If we are not active as part of a whole, working toward a higher goal, we will deteriorate inwardly and outwardly. Only if our hearts are in a task greater than ourselves will we thrive in earthly matters too. Society will deteriorate, physically and spiritually, unless each of its members has a task to fulfill for the sake of the common good, for creation, for God.*
>
> —Christoph Blumhardt

you and *your* in the English language can be either singular or plural, we automatically tend to individualize it. I will shine my light alone. While it can accurately be interpreted to mean that we should each shine our individual lights, Jesus was talking to a large crowd giving his Sermon on the Mount when he said those words and used the plural tense of *you*. In fact, it would probably be more accurate if we used the southern slang, "y'all" in the passage. All y'all, let your lights so shine together before men that they might see y'all's good deeds and glorify y'all's Father in heaven. The listeners probably imagined more of a raging bonfire than a little candle. In fact, he had told them they would be like a "city set on a hill" (Matt. 5:16).

I remember driving through the desert of Arizona at dusk and seeing Phoenix on the horizon. It glowed brightly and beautifully, not at all like a single, little candle. It was a magnificent sight. While we don't have hills in the city of Chicago, I am always stunned by the beauty of the city skyline at night. It is glorious. Many lights together create a glorious glow.

The lesson is obvious. When we all put our candles together and act together in community, the world will indeed see our good deeds and give glory to God. We can do so much more when we come together in community than we can one by one. Together, we can ignite a fire that can transform an entire community.

Another song that captured my passion as a child was this one: "I will make you fishers of men, fishers of men, fishers of men. I will make you fishers of men, if you follow me." Jesus was calling his disciples to follow him in Matthew 4 when he said, "Follow me and I will make you fishers of men." We personalized the song by pretending we had a rod and reel in our hands. We made an imaginary cast every time we sang the word *fishers* and reeled it in on the word *men*.

Of course, Jesus' disciples didn't fish with fishing rods; they fished with nets. Fishing with nets is not something you do by yourself. The disciples would have imagined joining others to stand at their place in a big net that God was spreading across the world. Drawing in the least and the lost to Christ is done together with others. It is in community that we draw people to Christ. Jesus was teaching a network model of caring for people.

The Network Model

When I began working in East Garfield Park on the west side of Chicago, I went door to door to get to know my neighbors. I asked them what they liked about the neighborhood and what their biggest challenges were. They loved the boulevards and the trees, the close proximity to parks and the transit trains. But almost unanimously they were concerned for their children. The kids weren't safe to play outside because of the perpetual violence of gang warfare and drug dealing.

In response to their concerns, I hired Bill and Marcie Curry to start a youth and family program in the community. Bill is a great strategic thinker and was concerned about the constant turnover of volunteers who mentor youth. Individual mentoring relationships were popular among youth programs, but there was a problem. Volunteers would come in from outside the community to lead summer programs for the kids. The kids would get attached to them and would weep as they said goodbye, knowing they would probably never see their new friends again. Tutors would commit for a semester of their school year, or until their job called them to another location. While we at Breakthrough appreciated their help for a season, the hearts of the kids were broken over and over again. With each new mentor, the kids' ability to entrust themselves to another mentor lessened, and mentors often left feeling badly about having to sever their relationships and leave the kids to start over with a new mentor.

Bill studied mentoring and learned that if mentoring relationships lasted less than a year, they could actually do more harm than good and that most mentoring relationships didn't last even that long. There had to be a better way.

Bill devised a new model for mentoring. Instead of a one-to-one mentoring program, he imagined what we have come to call the "network model."[1] We began to surround each of the kids in our program with multiple relationships with caring Christian adults: tutors, basketball coaches, Bible study leaders, baseball coaches, art teachers, and so forth. Each brings their unique gifts and personality into the lives of the children for as long as they are able to stay involved. Their mentoring relationships are supplemented by staff members and key volunteers who are involved in the lives of the children for the long haul.

When one of the volunteers gets called to another location, the personal loss for the child is tempered because the child is still surrounded by many friendly fans and supporters. Rather than asking the child to adjust to a new mentor, the new volunteer is the one who adjusts as he or she begins to fit into the network of support that is stable and consistent in the life of the child.

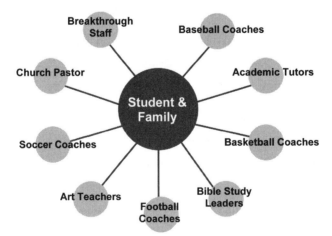

At the beginning of every school year, we give our students a blank relationship network form and ask them to enter names in their network of support. At the end of the year, we ask them again, and we measure how many more relationships they have established.

With this approach, we are not only building skills in the lives of our youth, but as we each bring our own networks into the lives of the children, we provide them with access to opportunity.

Sasha was a bright student who decided to join a Breakthrough girls' basketball team, not so much because she liked basketball, but because she liked being around the Breakthrough staff and volunteers. One of her volunteer basketball coaches was impressed by her potential. He knew an assistant principal at one of the better high schools in Chicago, St. Ignatius High School. Through his influence, Sasha was given the opportunity to enroll at St. Ignatius as a freshman. She finished her four years with honors, winning the Music Student of the Year award as a senior. After graduation she was accepted at VanderCook School of Music, where she is now studying to be a music teacher. A school in the community has already committed to hire her to teach music upon her graduation.

It is very unlikely that Sasha would have had these opportunities if she had not been introduced to the volunteer basketball coach who brought with him his network. In our community where fewer than 5 percent of the residents have graduated from college, Sasha is on track to get a college education and achieve a fulfilling and life-sustaining career because someone in her network gave her access to opportunity.

Bill Curry illustrates the power of the network with a story about learning to fish. His father taught him how to cast a rod and reel until Bill got very skilled at it, but there was a problem. Bill wasn't catching any fish. He wasn't catching fish because his father was teaching him how to fish in his driveway. It wasn't until one morning when his father and uncle loaded him into the car and went to the lake, that he actually

Tony

"Dogs should be free," Tony always shouted. Any conversation with him involved shouting back within inches of his World War II damaged ears. Getting that close was a challenge for me because it meant I had to hold my breath to keep from inhaling one of the most noxious odors imaginable.

"Can I take your dog for a walk?"

"Rocky? You want to take Rocky for a walk?" I looked at my beloved German shepherd and wondered how he would get along with the other three shepherds that sat patiently at Tony's side.

Tony nodded.

I shrugged. "Okay, if you think they'll get along."

"What?"

I leaned closer and yelled, "I said, okay, if you think they'll get along."

Tony grabbed Rocky's leash and herded all four dogs happily down the sidewalk as he slowly pushed his overflowing shopping cart along behind.

Tony was an accepted fixture in our upscale neighborhood. His long, bushy, gray hair, wind-burned face, and matted beard had earned him the nickname Santa Claus. It was rumored that he had a graduate degree from the University of Chicago and read *The Wall Street Journal* every day.

Tony stayed with us for awhile after both of his legs were broken under the wheels of a city bus. But as soon as he could shuffle behind his cart, he was out the door. Now, he only dropped by to check on his bags of stuff he had left in our garage and to visit Rocky. "Dogs should be free," he'd always say, shaking his grizzled head.

This wasn't the first time he had taken Rocky for a walk, but this time was different. He didn't return that afternoon . . . or the next day. Soon the walk had turned into a two-week dog napping, and I was frantic. Where was my dog? Where was Tony? Had he been mugged? Was his body chilling in the city morgue? Hoping for some clue to where he might have gone, I sorted through the bags he left behind and found hundreds of dollars in cash and checks but no clues to his whereabouts.

I cruised the streets and walked the parks, until one day, I located Tony in the park along the lakefront with my dog, Rocky, frolicking in his freedom.

experienced the joy of catching fish. He needed to have access to the lake in order to enjoy fishing.

You can imagine how disheartening it can be for youth in our neighborhood to learn skills when they don't have access to opportunities to use their skills. If they believe that getting an education or learning a new skill won't make a difference because they will never be able to get into a good school or use their skills to their advantage, they lose interest and eventually quit trying to excel academically or in any other endeavor. While we acknowledge the importance of helping young people build their skills in reading, science, music, and math, it is their network that provides them with the necessary links to opportunity.

Most of us can point to people in our lives who

have helped us to get into good schools or have linked us to jobs and other opportunities. In our neighborhood, where relationships to people outside of the community are often limited, it is this network of linkages that opens the doors for their future development.

We have expanded this model throughout our entire ministry. Men and women who come to our homeless shelters are similarly surrounded by multiple relationships with staff and volunteers. They have several case managers, healthcare professionals, a job trainer, a housing specialist, a spiritual director, and many relationships with volunteers who provide computer training, serve meals regularly, lead life-skill groups, or just sit and play bingo with them. When they come to Breakthrough, they are surrounded with many positive relationships with caring Christians who are there to love them with the love of Christ.

This approach to community development is dependent upon lots of volunteers who will join a movement to make a difference in the community. More than a thousand volunteers come to Breakthrough each month to become part of the network of support for the children in our programs and the men and women in our housing programs. Each brings his or her unique set of gifts to the Breakthrough network. Together we cast a net of compassion and support across the community. When we share the load, none of us is overly burdened with the needs of people who are experiencing the crushing challenges of poverty. We don't do it alone.

In Psalm 27, David wrote, "Though my father and mother forsake me, the LORD will receive me." The Hebrew word for "receive," *acaph*, means to be gathered into association with others. This is a beautiful picture of what should happen for those who have been cast aside by friends, family, and society. The forsaken will be "gathered in" by the Lord. Of course, God uses the church, the body of Christ on earth, to act as the ingathering arms of the Lord, to bring people into association with the family of God where they can experience God's love and be nurtured to new life. Together, we "gather in" those who have been left at the margins.

It is also important to recognize that those who come from outside a community must learn to listen to and partner with those who are already doing good work in the community. If you enter a neighborhood with even a hint of paternalism or a sense of superiority, it will be quickly recognized and rejected by those who have been faithfully serving in a community for years. Aboriginal activist, Lilla Watson, spoke very frankly about how important our attitude is when she said, "If you have come here to help me, you are wasting your time. But if you have come because your liberation is bound up with mine, then let us work together."[2]

We Can't Do It Alone

Issues of poverty are convoluted and complex. Addressing poverty is not something we can do by ourselves: It necessitates that we join, movements for change. God wires us with compassion for specific issues and empowers us to join with like-minded people to change the status quo. Whether it be human trafficking, AIDS orphans in Africa, single moms and the unborn, those in prison, impoverished urban dwellers, the elderly, or the poor next door, we are drawn to issues that can be changed only by our combined efforts.

Root causes of poverty are almost always systemic in nature. More than thirteen million children in the United States—18 percent of all children—live in families with incomes below the federal poverty level—22,050 dollars a year for a family of four. Research shows that, on average, families need an income of about twice that level to cover basic expenses. Using this standard, 39 percent of children in the U.S. live in low-income families.[3]

While we can debate whether some adults living in poverty may have brought their situation on themselves because of their choices, there is no debate that children living in poverty have not chosen their situation. These children will grow into adulthood with little opportunity unless the church steps up to the plate and extends a helping hand.

In Chicago, between September 2007 and December 2008, more than five hundred Chicago public school students were shot.[4] These children and their parents live in constant fear of violence.

The grammar schools in our community are ranked the lowest in the state because students begin the first day of kindergarten without knowing basic colors, how to count to twenty, or basic social skills. Out of 2,265 total grammar schools in Illinois, the four grammar schools closest to Breakthrough are all ranked in the bottom one hundred.

The University of Chicago's study of our local grammar schools shows that only 50 percent of students go on to graduate from high school, and over 52 percent of the students (2002–2007) had an F in reading or math during their freshman year. Most of the eighth graders matriculated to significantly underperforming high schools where a diploma means little externally.

At our local high school, students in 2008 scored an average of 5.8 in reading and 3.2 in math (out of a possible one hundred). In a school where attendance alone will get you a D, the graduation rate is less than 40 percent, and the school is ranked six hundredth of the 604 high school in Illinois.[5]

There are one hundred seventy days in a school year in Chicago. The average number of days missed by students at John Marshall High School is ninety-five. Like Bill's experience of the exasperation of fishing in the driveway without access to a lake, young people in our community don't value education because they are not seeing their friends succeeding academically, nor do they see the rewards of doing so. They don't see how school attendance will provide access to opportunity; so, why bother? We need to think creatively about how to educate our children in the city and join together to lift this boulder of inadequate education from the backs of our children and their parents. We need to join a movement that will reform our system of public education in urban neighborhoods.

There are many other issues that need to be addressed in order to change the systems that keep people locked in poverty. Healthcare is a tremendous issue in our urban community. If we continue to associate healthcare with employment, those who cannot find work are dependent upon emergency rooms and public health clinics for their health needs. Needless to say, they neglect preventative measures that grow to eventually become even more expensive to our systems of public health. One of our local hospitals was closed after losing millions of dollars each year because community residents were using the emergency room for their primary health care needs. Beyond the healthcare debate in the public sector, Christians should be leading the charge in caring for the physical health and well-being of the people we are called to love.

A doctor who works in one of our clinics told me how difficult it is for him when he is sitting across from someone in excruciating pain who needs a root canal, and he has nowhere to send him. Or he is treating someone who is regularly hallucinating and needs a simple five-dollar prescription to which he has no access.

We need help. We need your strategic thinking, your ideas, your resources, both financially and personally, in order to provide a network of care around so many who are in pain.

The Greater Chicago Food Depository, along with LaSalle Bank, conducted research and identified our community, East Garfield Park, as a "food desert." Local residents have little or no access to healthy food options. No major grocery store exists in the community, while many corner stores supply the neighborhood children with individual-sized sugar-loaded snack foods. Basics such as milk and bread are more expensive than at upscale grocers, and shops that sell food are more likely to sell alcohol and cigarettes than fresh produce.[6] It is easier to get illegal drugs than a salad in our community.

We need help to establish connections to sources for fresh produce and to develop urban vegetable gardens. One of our volunteers took it upon herself to purchase hundreds of dollars' worth of fresh fruit every week for the kids in our after-school program. We were skeptical at first, wondering if the kids would really eat the fruit, but they gobbled it up, some of them experiencing for the first time the joy of eating blueberries, apricots, and kiwi.

A group of women from a Chicago suburb joined together to create a library for the children in our programs. They networked their friends to purchase thousands of children's books, purchased and set up the shelves, carpeted the floor, and equipped the room with chairs, tables, and computers. Not only did they meet a real need for the children in our community, but they had fun doing it.

David Anderson, executive director of the Lydia Home Association, developed the Safe Families program. Safe Families is a network of families that have agreed to temporarily take in the children of families who are in distress, many of them due to homelessness or other crisis. Each year, Safe Families provides refuge to more than a thousand children who would otherwise be placed in the foster care system. By linking healthy, safe families with families in crisis, Safe Families is building a safety net around children who might otherwise be abused, neglected, or lost in the mammoth government bureaucracy of children's services.

If the church isolates itself from relating in tangible ways with those who have been marginalized by society, we miss something essential about what it means to know who God is. All people are created in God's image and reflect something of the wisdom and character of God to us. Most Christians genuinely want to know God better, and joining a movement for change that brings us into contact with those in need is one important way to know God. God is a God of love for all people. When we express that same kind of love, we begin to experience God's heart. We take our place on the net alongside people who struggle, and together we draw others into the love of God.

You will meet wonderful people in this movement to care for the poor, people who have found meaning beyond the drudgery of living for their paychecks or their next purchase. These are people who are challenging the status quo. They are a cadre of creative people who are networking their friends to make a difference. They have taken their place on the net, reworking the fabric of the shalom of God. They are the light of the world, a city on a hill that cannot be hidden.

The Breakthrough of Racial Understanding

I was driving home from Trinity International University to my home in Chicago one hot, humid night when I saw a police car light up behind me. I suddenly remembered I had forgotten to put the renewal sticker on my license plate. It was on my desk at home. I wasn't worried. I knew the routine: "I'm sorry, Officer," I would say. "I have my sticker at home. I will go home immediately and put it on." He would smile and nod understandingly, perhaps give me a little warning, and send me on my way. Police officers were my friends. They were there to serve and protect me.

But this time it was different. Peering into my car, the policeman glared at the five African-American men crammed

> Our attitudes toward things like race or gender operate on two levels . . . our conscious attitudes . . . what we choose to believe and our unconscious attitudes, the immediate, automatic associations that tumble out before we've even had time to think.
>
> —Malcolm Gladwell

into my '85 Chevy Caprice. He barked an order for me to step out and move to the rear of the car. "Put your hands on the car," he demanded gruffly. "What are you doing here? Where are you coming from? Where are you going?" I was shocked and totally unprepared for the demeaning altercation. I had never been treated with such disrespect by a police officer.

I stumbled over myself, trying to explain that I was the director of a ministry and the guys in my car were coming from a job in Deerfield where they had worked all day to move a library from one building to another. He questioned me until he finally bought my story. Only then did his attitude toward me change. What if I wouldn't have had an explanation other than I was with my friends, and we were going for a joy ride? I felt terribly frightened and vulnerable. What if I was truly like the men in the car? How could I live with that constant disdain? How would I not lash out in anger at a system that judged me only on the basis of my skin?

That experience was the first time I felt a little of what people in our community call "driving while black." I have since learned that being stopped and questioned by the police for no apparent reason is common for African-Americans. There are entire neighborhoods that some of my friends avoid because they feel they will surely be stopped and questioned.

Lack of Awareness

I was quite unaware of the prejudicial ways people of color are treated and the pervasiveness of racism until I came into trusted relationships with people of color who began to educate me about their experiences. They tell me about being followed around in stores, about having racial slurs hurled at them, about not being able to get jobs and apartments, about not knowing if rebuffs are based on their race or some other factor, of getting passed by for promotions, of struggling to get into good schools, of living constantly with the ever-present awareness that the color of their skin affects nearly everything in their lives every minute of the day.

Living in a community in which I am a minority has caused me to become increasingly aware of my need to grow in my understanding of the history and present state of race relations. I have watched many of my Wheaton College students and our Breakthrough volunteers experience transformation as they have embarked on the painful journey of racial understanding. Facing the systemic evil of racism in our culture can be shocking for those of us who have lived in ethnic isolation. And coming face-to-face with our own prejudice can shake us to the core.

Educator John Erskine has said we have a "moral obligation to be intelligent."[1] It is not okay for us to bury our heads in the sand and pretend racism doesn't exist when it has such a devastating effect on so many Americans. Yet, many, if not most, of us who are of European descent continue to isolate ourselves from having to do the tough work of racial understanding and justice. When we accept the invitation to get to know people with backgrounds different from our own, and when we begin to love one another with the love of Christ, our hearts are broken by the stories of racial injustice experienced by our friends.

Those of us who are white in America have not been forced to learn about other cultures. We see the world through ethnocentric lenses. Even our history books have excluded large portions of history that would educate us about the influence and accomplishments of people of color. We can live in our white bubble our entire lives and be unaware that our brothers and sisters across town or down the street struggle every day with experiences of racism and prejudice.

St. Augustine has been credited with saying, "The world is a book and those who do not travel read only one page."[2] Since people of all races and nationalities are created in the image of God, those of us who figuratively do not travel outside of our own race are missing a whole lot of the experience of the colorful mosaic of God's image. We read only one page of who God is.

Denial

"But I'm not a racist." Of course, if we remain unaware, we will tend to deny that we maintain any bias toward people who are not like us. We think we are viewing and treating all people equally simply because we don't know what we don't know.

We run a Christmas store every year at Breakthrough. We gather gifts from our donors and volunteers and allow people from the community and the residents of our shelters to buy gifts at a greatly discounted rate or with "Breakthrough Bucks" that they earn by doing service projects. We have found this is the most dignifying way for our program participants and community residents to purchase and receive Christmas gifts.

One year, as we were planning for the store, we were discussing how we would engage people from the community who are predominately African-American along with volunteers from a church group who would be coming from a white suburb. One of our staff members suggested the people from the community could take care of preparing and serving the food while the suburban white folks could run the operations of the store.

One of our black staff leaders was outraged. "There you go again!" she proclaimed. "Let the white people manage the store and collect the money, and put the blacks in the kitchen!" We hadn't set out to demean black people, but the unconscious bias—the subtle presumption of who would fit where best—was lurking beneath the surface. We didn't even realize it.

Regardless of our intent, the consequences are hurtful. We need to urge people around us to challenge us and call us out on our blind spots. We need to be prepared to listen without trying to defend ourselves. Instead, people of color often experience our ignorance without comment, perhaps having given up on ever seeing change or doubting that we care enough to change, perhaps even fearing that our denial and defense would further patronize them.

I hear white students voice their frustration with being confronted about racism. "I understand that slavery was a terrible thing, but that's a thing of the past. My family doesn't own slaves, and I resent being held responsible for something that happened years ago." As they read about the current status of segregation and inequality in our public school systems, the practices of exclusion by landlords and loan officers, and the absence of networks that would link people of color to jobs with a living wage, they begin to realize that their experience as whites is vastly different from that of most people of color, and they begin to own the fact that their privilege has been obtained at a price. Generations of family wealth and the foundations of the opportunities they continue to enjoy were built with free labor on stolen land. Their denial begins to break down, and they usually fall into disturbed silence.

White Privilege

One of our African-American leaders called a pizza restaurant to order lunch for a staff meeting and was informed the restaurant did not take credit cards. Knowing they had taken credit in the past, a white staff member called just a few minutes later and was able to charge the meal.

The scales begin to fall from our eyes as we come to understand white privilege. One of the most helpful articles I have found on this is Peggy McIntosh's classic paper titled "Unpacking the Invisible Knapsack."[3] In it she outlines privileges that whites experience that others don't. As a white person, I can be assured that I can rent or purchase a home that I can afford wherever I want to live. I don't have to worry about being followed around in stores or having my method of payment questioned. My children will learn from history books that explain the contributions of people who look like them. I can find the hair products that I need in the supermarket. I don't have to worry that people will shun my children or call them names. I can dress casually and not worry that I will be treated differently.

We have gathered groups of people together regularly at Breakthrough to form culture circles for the purpose of learning from one another about our experiences and understanding of race. After meeting together three or four times, we do the "privilege exercise" in which we ask a set of questions regarding the participants' childhood experiences based on the list from Peggy McIntosh's article. Participants take a step to the right or the left depending on their answers to the questions.

The result is always sobering. Inevitably, by the end of the exercise, there is a visible divide based upon race. Those of European descent can't deny white privilege, and we are forced to look at the systems in place that have oppressed our brothers and sisters. This is new and unfamiliar territory for us. Many turn away at this point because the journey of racial justice begins to get difficult. This is the stage when we whites begin to feel frustrated, misunderstood, and confused.

Dissonance

"It is what it is. I can't help the fact that I'm white. What do you want me to do about it? I didn't choose to be born white. It's not my fault." We get defensive and perhaps even angry. We are frightened that we are losing control. Our neatly crafted worldview is beginning to crack, and we don't know what we will become.

We feel perplexed by the insidious way in which we have been co-opted by a system that has affirmed our superiority, and that has sanctioned our way of doing things as the best way, the right way. We feel embarrassed that we have lived so long in ignorance, or we may even become aggressive, trying to remove ourselves from the uncomfortable tension. We are fearful that we will be confronted, that we will have to change.

Eventually those who persist through this stage of the journey will begin to feel grief. Tears are shed. Emotions run deep. We are led to repent of the many ways "our people" have oppressed others. We become aware of the great systemic sin of racism and we are broken.

Some people struggle with the idea of repenting for sins they didn't personally commit. "Why?" they ask. "I never did it! None of my ancestors owned slaves." But there are rich biblical examples of identification in repentance. Even though Nehemiah probably was not personally guilty, he prayed, "I confess the sins we Israelites, including myself and my father's house, have committed against you. We have acted very wickedly toward you. We have not obeyed the commands, decrees and laws you gave your servant Moses" (Neh. 1:6–7).

Similarly Daniel prayed, "We have sinned and done wrong. We have been wicked and have rebelled; we have turned away from your commands and laws. We have not listened to your servants the prophets, who spoke in your name to our kings, our princes and our fathers, and to all the people of the land" (Dan. 9:5–6).

In both cases, these holy prophets repented whether or not they personally participated in or benefited from the sins of their ancestors and fellow Hebrews. How much more should we be willing to express repentance for the things done by our own people groups when we have benefited from a long history of policies and legislation that have excluded so many people from equal opportunity?

God honors sincere prayers of repentance.

Grief and Repentance

"We just want you to acknowledge it, that's all. Just acknowledge the injustice toward people of color in this country. Admit to the history of oppression and that you are still benefitting from it. We just want to know that you understand and that you care. If church leaders would just lead the people of God to repentance, it would mean so much to us. Is that too much to ask?" He spoke with passion on the verge of tears after sitting in on one of my workshops about race. He had recently emigrated from Nigeria, so he didn't even have an ancestry of slavery in his background. But he had experienced enough prejudice in his short time in America to be indignant and exasperated by the insensitivity he had experienced from whites.

Leading the people of God to repentance is exactly what it will take for racism to be overcome. For repentance to be genuine, we must first become aware that there is a problem, accept responsibility for our participation in the perpetuation of the problem, and acknowledge that sin is corporate as well as individual.

True repentance involves a change in direction, a commitment to join with others to right the wrongs that have oppressed people, a decision to mourn with those who mourn and weep with those who weep, a determination to stay in the journey toward racial justice despite the costs to our egos and to our sense of power and identity. We commit ourselves to be learners and to submit ourselves to leaders and teachers who can educate us about race. We commit ourselves to love one another as Christ has loved us, laying down our lives for one another.

Joseph Barndt, in his book *Dismantling Racism*, tells of an experience he had in 1966 while marching with Stokely Carmichael. As a white man, he had aligned himself with the leaders of the civil rights movement and had joined the cause by marching for racial justice. His feelings were hurt when someone yelled at him from the crowd and said, "White man, go home and free your own people!" He said he pondered those words and realized that, indeed, the most productive thing he could do for the cause of racial equality was to work for change among his own people, to free his own people.[4]

Racism is a scourge on all of us. We are not free when anyone in our society is oppressed by racially biased policies and practices, nor are we free when "our people" are shackled by ignorance and prejudice.

Genuine Cross-Cultural Relationships

The way to freedom is through honest reconciling of cross-cultural relationships. When Jesus and his disciples were on their way from Judea to Galilee, John reported that Jesus needed to go through Samaria (John 4). He didn't say he wanted to go through Samaria, or it would be nice to go through Samaria. He needed to go through Samaria, even though the Jews usually avoided this more direct route in favor of the longer, eastern route through Peraea.

The Samaritans were despised by the Jews, and this animosity contributed to the kind of strife Jesus and his disciples experienced on another trip when they were not welcomed in a Samaritan village, and the irate disciples said, "Lord, do you want us to call fire down from heaven to destroy them?" (Luke 9:54). Jesus rebuked them.

But on this trip, Jesus needed to go through Samaria to meet a troubled woman at Jacob's well. His disciples were shocked by Jesus' audacity to cross boundaries of race and gender. Jesus didn't speak to the woman about racial harmony. He just became her friend. He asked her questions. He spoke to her of living water that would heal and transform her brokenness. His love broke through the barriers and freed her from her shame.

Malcolm Gladwell describes a test developed by Harvard researchers called the Implicit Association Test. The test, which is available online, flashes pictures of people on the screen and requires that you quickly tap a left or right key if you associate the face with being good or bad. Gladwell writes, "The disturbing thing about this test is that it shows that our unconscious attitudes may be utterly incompatible with our stated values. As it turns out, for example, of the fifty thousand African-Americans who have taken the Race IAT so far, about half of them have stronger associations with whites than with blacks. How could we not? We live in North America, where we are surrounded every day by cultural messages linking white with good."[5]

The researchers found that no matter how hard we try, we cannot will or think away our prejudices. The only thing that has been found to break down walls of prejudice is multiple associations with people that cross racial lines. The more interactions we have with people who are different from us, the less likely we are to stereotype and prejudge them.

Racial tensions in the U.S. bubbled to the surface during President Barack Obama's run for the White House. Some people assumed that because of his name, he was a Muslim. Images of fried chicken, watermelon, and monkeys began to appear. Christians at the Family

Research Council's Value Voters Summit sold boxes of Obama Waffles that pictured a cartoon image of Obama with popping eyes and big thick lips and another image of him in Arab headdress. These kinds of associations revealed unjust fear and prejudice based on the color of Obama's skin.

The only way to rid ourselves of these racist demons is to engage intentionally in multiple cross-cultural relationships. One of the ways we have tried to bridge the racial divide at Breakthrough is through culture circles, as mentioned earlier in this chapter. We merge people from very different backgrounds in small groups and for eight weeks, we meet to engage in discussions about race. We read material about historical and current oppressive policies and practices and study the advantages of white privilege. We hear about personal experiences of racism from people who have lived with prejudice all of their lives.

Participants in these groups report radical transformation in their perspectives. Even people of color are awakened to their own experiences of racism as they are given the opportunity to give voice to their thoughts and feelings. A woman in one of our groups began to notice that she was followed around the store when she shopped. She hadn't realized that this didn't happen to the whites who shopped in the same store.

If you are living in social isolation, associating only with people who are like you, I think Jesus would issue an invitation to you to follow him to Samaria, to a place beyond your comfort zone, perhaps across town or to the nearest city, to a place where you can meet people who are struggling to live under oppressive systems of prejudice and injustice. You need to go there to experience healing relationships. Perhaps you will find that Jesus is already there, sitting at the well, waiting for you.

Do Something 13

Every once in awhile, we need to be challenged to change our lives. We need a good kick in the pants. We need someone to tell us it is time to get up off the couch, turn off the TV, stop Tweeting and Facebooking, and do something.

I hope you have been challenged to see that as Christians, we don't really have an option about caring for the poor. Scripture teaches it. Jesus modeled it. The Law required it. And grace invites us to it. God wants to give us something through our relationships with the poor that is for our good as well as for the good of the oppressed.

So where do we start? Here are a few suggestions.

> *Even the little pigs grunt when the old boar suffers.*
> —Selma Lagerlöf

The Red Dot: Where Are You Now?

Start with a frank assessment of your present situation. Most shopping malls have maps encased in glass to help us find our way. The key to reading the map is to find the red dot with the declaration, "You Are Here." If we can locate where we are, we have a better chance of knowing how to get to where we want to be. How are you doing presently in expressing the love of Christ to people who are in difficult situations? Get out a journal and notebook, set aside a few quiet hours and answer the following questions:

1. When was the last time you shared a meal with a poor person?
2. How much money have you contributed in the past year to care for the poor?
3. What cause or causes are you presently actively engaged in?
4. How many people in your network are from races and socioeconomic groups that are different from yours?
5. What is stopping you from getting more involved in a movement that is working for compassion and justice?

Your Passion: What Moves You?

Once you have a good idea of where you are, you can start asking yourself questions that will reveal the area of service to which God is calling you.

What are the issues you care about? What breaks your heart, makes you cry, makes you feel? Is it children? The mentally ill? The elderly? Single mothers? Is there an issue that has evidenced itself in your family?

I care about arthritis because my father suffered with it. I care about single moms because my daughter has become one. I care about kids in the city because my kids were raised in the city, and many of their friends have been incarcerated, are living in dire circumstances, or have lost their lives to street violence. I care about the homeless because many of them have become my friends.

What issues matter most to you? Education? Healthcare? Economic development? Housing? Nutrition? Hunger? What do you think needs to be changed in order for everyone to have equal opportunity? What moves you emotionally? Remember that theologian Frederick Buechner said, "The place God calls you to is the place where your deep gladness and the world's deep hunger meet."[1] What makes you glad?

I am made glad by seeing underdogs turn their lives around. I love to see people who have never had hope for their future begin to dream. I love to develop leaders. I love to see people operate in their area of gift-edness. I love to build and create things. It makes me glad. Where does your deep gladness meet the world's deep hunger?

Pray for Guidance: Where Is God Leading You?

Take time to sit in prayer with God, affirming your openness to making changes in your life as the Spirit directs you.

If there is any hint of guilt or self-condemnation, lay it at Jesus' feet and know that he loves you. Imagine Jesus is picking up a towel and washing your feet. Look into his eyes and feel his love for you just as you are. There is nothing you can do to make God love you more. Jesus does not require your acts of service to win his love. He just invites you to take up the towel and follow him because he loves you. This is not a burden. It's an adventure.

Where is God leading you? Ask him to give you a vision for what you are being called to. Spend thirty minutes in uninterrupted silence, letting God speak to you through your thoughts.

Write Down Your Vision: Where Are You Going?

What would your life look like if you used your gifts and abilities to care for the poor? Can you picture it? Write about it in as much detail as you can. Draw or paint an image of yourself carrying out your vision. What will you be doing five years from now that will leave your mark on the world? What would you like to be said of you at your funeral? Write it down. Read it out loud.

Build Your Plan

What do you need to do now to move you toward your goal? Build a five-year plan and break it down into years, quarters, weeks, and days. Schedule appointments with God on your calendar in order to check in on how you are doing in carrying out the plan God has given you.

Bill Lutes, former program manager for Wisconsin Public Radio, wrote, "All one can do is make little beginnings, to try to do 'the next right thing.'" What is the next right thing for you to do? What do you need to focus on? What do you need to cut out? What do you need to prioritize?

Share Your Plan with a Friend

Remember, this is not something you can do by yourself. You need others to join you. Invite them into your plan. Ask for their help. Ask a trusted friend to hold you accountable.

Execute

Nike says it best: "Just do it!" Your life will become so much more meaningful when you begin to spend it on behalf of others. I don't know anyone who has given their time, talent, and treasure to care for the poor who regrets it. Instead, I have seen people come alive as they have taken up their cross and let themselves be broken and spilled out for others.

Dream Big

Big problems need big solutions. There is no end to the opportunities to make an impact on alleviating poverty. While we always need to provide emergency housing and personal care for people who fall through the cracks, there are emerging enterprise initiatives that stretch our imagination and creativity with new ways of empowering people. Can you imagine how much more dignifying it would be for the men and women in our shelters to be given support in starting their own businesses rather than being passive recipients of our charity?

Two women in one of our shelters have started their own business, sewing bags with a couple of donated sewing machines and recycled clothing they find in our clothing room. They sell their handmade products online (etsy.com). Others know how to braid hair or build furniture. We have met many wonderful artists and musicians who, with a little help, could support themselves with their own skills.

Jan Martinez founded Christ Kitchen in Spokane, Washington, to empower women in poverty. She brings church women together across socioeconomic barriers. They share the love Christ with one another while bagging soup beans, corn bread mix, and other delicious treats. The women learn job skills and experience the reciprocity of Christ's love while creating a beautiful selection of food baskets.[2]

Sweet Misgivings is a bakery in Chicago that hires homeless people with HIV and other disabilities to bake cookies, bread, and cupcakes and deliver them to business meetings and events. They sell their baked goods to restaurants and coffee shops and on their Web site.[3]

In our neighboring community, North Lawndale, where six out of ten adults have a criminal record, a creative program called Sweet Beginnings is training formerly incarcerated men to work as beekeepers. They tend hives and harvest honey and package it under the brand Beeline. Their skincare products, including body polisher and exfoliant, are available online and on the shelves of a local Whole Foods grocery store.[4]

In Milwaukee, Will Allen has developed an urban farming enterprise that grows salad greens and vegetables. He teaches workshops on worm composting, aquaponics construction, and other farm skills. "We need fifty million more people growing food," Allen told a *New York Times* magazine journalist, "on porches, in pots, in side yards . . . Chicago has 77,000 vacant lots."[5]

We can stretch our imaginations in creating new initiatives that bring about real change in the lives of people caught in the cycle of poverty, knowing we can never out-love or out-dream God. God "is able to do immeasurably more than all we ask or imagine, according to his power that is at work within us" (Eph. 3:20).

Together We Can Make a Difference

There is hope for the man at my car window and for the many others who are living under bridges and in shelters throughout our country. While dropping a few dollars in a dirty cup can be a start and perhaps a necessary expression of our love for God and people, it doesn't have to end there. Together we can make an impact on the forgotten world of the man at my window by addressing the root causes: poverty, addiction, and isolation. We can spread the net of God's love by joining together to reweave the fabric of a broken world.

Everyone is important. You are important. Will you take your place in the network of shalom that God is casting over the broken systems of the world that toss people aside? The invitation to come alongside the poor is not just for the likes of Mother Teresa, St. Francis of Assisi, and George Müller. It is for you. Welcome to the journey. You will never be the same.

Notes

Chapter 1

1. Bill Hybels, *Holy Discontent: Fueling the Fire That Ignites Personal Vision* (Grand Rapids, Mich.: Zondervan, 2007).

2. All Great Quotes, http://www.allgreatquotes.com/love_quotes254.shtml.

3. New America Media, "Chicago's Black Communities Some of City's Deadliest," http://news.newamericamedia.org/news/view_article.html?article_id=f865084da09ec0 7d4d6f85de1f8abfd0.

4. The Chicago Reporter, "The Wish List," http://www.chicagoreporter.com/ index.php/c/Sidebars/d/The_wish_list.

Chapter 2

1. "I Don't Think About It," words and music by Sue Fabisch and Ilene Angel. © 2003 New Angel Music. (ASCAP). Administered by Mandalay Way Music. Recorded by Emily Osment, 2007, *Disney Radio Jams 10*.

2. Henry Blackaby, Richard Blackaby, and Claude King, *Experiencing God: Knowing and Doing the Will of God* (Nashville, Tenn.: B&H, 2008), 69.

3. One, "Bono's Acceptance Speech," http://action.one.org/blog/?p=454&t=& gclid=CNyNr4GEj5gCFQHHGod0wcEDg.

Chapter 3

1. This number comes from *The Poverty and Justice Bible* (New York: American Bible Society, 2008). While a few of the highlighted passages do not seem to relate to either poverty or justice, most are very explicit. How many hundreds of times does God need to express his deep concern for the poor before we recognize their importance to him?

2. "Broken and Spilled Out," words by Gloria Gaither, music by Bill George, © 1984 Gaither Music Co./Yellow House Music. All rights reserved. Used by permission.

Chapter 4

1. Walter Rauschenbusch, *Christianity and the Social Crisis* (London: Macmillan, 1907).

2. Ibid., xiii.

3. Ibid., 149.

4. Iain H. Murray, *The Puritan Hope: Revival and the Interpretation of Prophecy* (Carlisle, Pa.: The Banner of Truth Trust, 1971), 198.

5. John Stott, *Human Rights & Human Wrongs: Major Issues for a New Century* (Grand Rapids, Mich.: Baker Books, 1999), 22, quoting George M. Marsden, *Fundamentalism and American Culture* (New York: Oxford University Press, 1980), 85–93.

6. George M. Marsden, *Fundamentalism and American Culture* (New York: Oxford University Press, 2006), 36–37.

7. Stott, *Human Rights*, 23–24, quoting David O. Moberg, *The Great Reversal* (Milton Keynes, UK: Scripture Union, 1973), 184.

8. Carl Ellis, *Free at Last?: The Gospel in the African-American Experience* (Downers Grove, Ill.: InterVarsity, 1996), 81.

9. ———, "The Sovereignty of God and Ethnic-Based Suffering," in John Piper and Justin Taylor, *Suffering and the Sovereignty of God* (Wheaton, Ill.: Crossway, 2006), 138–139.

10. Manya A. Brachear, "Rev. Bill Hybels: The Father of Willow Creek," *Chicago Tribune* (August 6, 2006), http://articles.chicagotribune.com/2006-08-06/news/0608060421_1_pastors-rev-bill-hybels-willow-creek-community-church/4.

Chapter 5

1. "Breakthrough Broke Through," words and music by Babbie Mason. © 2008 Babbie Mason. Written and performed for Breakthrough Urban Ministries' Breakaway Retreat, February 15, 2008. Used by permission, Babbie Mason.

2. Timothy C. Morgan, "Purpose Driven in Rwanda," *Christianity Today* (October 2005), http://www.christianitytoday.com/ct/2005/october/17.32.html.

3. Ibid., http://www.christianitytoday.com/ct/2005/october/17.32.html?start=2.

4. Ibid.

Chapter 6

1. Dr. Martin Luther King, Jr., adapted from "Letter from a Birmingham Jail," April 16, 1963. The actual quote is "I have almost reached the regrettable conclusion that the Negro's greatest stumbling block in his stride toward freedom is not the White Citizen's Council or the Ku Klux Klan, but the white moderate, who is more devoted to 'order' than to justice; who prefers a negative peace which is the absence of tension to a positive peace which is the presence of justice."

2. Cornelius Plantinga, Jr., *Not the Way It's Supposed to Be: A Breviary of Sin* (Grand Rapids, Mich.: Eerdmans, 1995), 10.

3. Timothy Keller, "Doing Justice" (Resurgence), 54 min., 22 sec.; MPEG, http://www.theresurgence.com/r_r_2006_session_eight_audio_keller.

4. Ibid.

5. Richard Rohr and John Bookser Feister, *Jesus' Plan for a New World: The Sermon on the Mount* (Cincinnati, Ohio: St. Anthony Messenger Press, 1996), 11.

6. Carl Ellis, "Bridging the Racial Divide" (lecture, Breakthrough Urban Ministries, Chicago, Ill., January 17, 2008).

7. Ibid.

Chapter 7

1. Wikipedia, "Participant Observation," http://en.wikipedia.org/wiki/Participant_observation.

2. Wayne Gordon, Christian Community Development Association, "The Eight Components of Christian Community Development," http://www.ccda.org/philosophy.

Chapter 8

1. A. J. Russell, *God Calling* (New York: Jove, 1978), 77.

2. Oswald Chambers, *My Utmost for His Highest* (Grand Rapids, Mich.: Discovery House, 2008), 165.

Chapter 9

1. The H2O Project, "The H2O Challenge," http://livingwater.theh2oproject.org/. See also World Vision, "Clean Water," http://donate.wvus.org/OA_HTML/xxwv2ibe CCtpSctDspRte.jsp?section=10373.

2. One, "Bono's Acceptance Speech," http://action.one.org/blog/?p=454&t=&gclid= CNyNr4GEj5gCFQHHGgod0wcEDg.

3. Generous Giving, "Stories & Testimonies," http://library.generousgiving.org/page.asp?sec=8&page=569.

4. Stanley Tam, *God Owns My Business* (Alberta, Canada: Horizon House Publishers, 1969), 25–37.

5. According to Illinois Legal Aid, "The Illinois Food Stamps Calculator," http://www.illinoislegalaid.org/index.cfm?fuseaction=home.dsp_content&content ID=871, the maximum amount for food stamps one person could receive would be two hundred dollars. Factors such as income, housing, and whether anyone else helps with "family" expenses reduce the actual amount from the maximum.

6. Christian Smith, Michael O. Emerson, Patricia Snell, *Passing the Plate: Why American Christians Don't Give Away More Money* (New York: Oxford University Press, 2008), 176.

7. Ibid., 145.

8. Ibid., 171.

9. Ibid., 34.

10. Ibid., 60.

11. Ibid., 25.

12. Ibid., 29.

13. DaveRamsey.com, http://www.daveramsey.com/. Dave Ramsey is a great resource for help with money management.

14. YouTube, "Catalyst Conference Dave Ramsey," http://www.youtube.com/watch?v=_eMs-LWg1EA.

15. T. A. Bryant, *Today's Dictionary of the Bible* (Minneapolis, Minn.: Bethany, 1983), 89.

Chapter 10

1. The Upper Room, www.upperroom.org. The *Examen*, a method of prayer developed by the Jesuits, provides five helpful steps; Thinkjesuit.org, http://www.thinkjesuit.org/sjcafe/Rummaging for God.doc.

2. Frederick Buechner, *Wishful Thinking: A Seeker's ABC* (San Francisco, Calif.: HarperOne, 1993), 119.

Chapter 11

1. Breakthrough Urban Ministries, "The Breakthrough Network Model," http://breakthrough.org/general/30/network-model.

2. Wikipedia, "Lilla Watson," http://en.wikipedia.org/wiki/Lilla_Watson.

3. National Center for Children in Poverty, "Child Poverty," http://www.nccp.org/topics/childpoverty.html.

4. "508 Chicago Kids Shot in Just 16 Months," *Chicago Sun-Times* (March 9, 2009), http://www.suntimes.com/news/commentary/1466791,CST-EDT-edit09.article.

5. Refer to School Digger, schooldigger.com, for more up-to-date information regarding school rankings.

6. Greater Chicago Food Depository, http://www.chicagosfoodbank.org; http://www.marigallagher.com/site_media/dynamic/project_files/Chicago_Food_Desert_Report.pdf.

Chapter 12

1. John Erskine, *The Moral Obligation to be Intelligent, and Other Essays* (Indianapolis, Ind.: Bobbs-Merrill Company Publishers, 1915), 3–32.

2. About.com, "Travel Quotations," http://honeymoons.about.com/cs/wordsofwisdom/a/TravelQuotes.htm.

3. Peggy McIntosh, "White Privilege: Unpacking the Invisible Knapsack," http://seac.org/readings/winter09/unpacking_knapsack.pdf.

4. Joseph Barndt, *Understanding and Dismantling Racism The Twenty-first Century Challenge to White America* (Minneapolis, Minn.: Fortress Press, 2007), 112–113.

5. Malcom Gladwell, *Blink: The Power of Thinking Without Thinking* (New York: Little, Brown and Company, 2005), 85.

Chapter 13

1. Frederick Buechner, *Wishful Thinking: A Seeker's ABC* (San Francisco, Calif.: HarperOne, 1993), 119.

2. Christ Kitchen, http://www.christkitchen.org/.

3. Sweet Miss Giving's, http://sweetmissgivings.com/.

4. Bee Line, http://www.beelinestore.com/.

5. Elizabeth Royte, "Street Farmer," *The New York Times* (July 1, 2009), http://www.nytimes.com/2009/07/05/magazine/05allen-t.html?_r=2&ref=magazine.